SURVIVING THE DIGITAL JUNGLE

What Every Executive Needs to Know About eCommerce and eBusiness

Jack Shaw

Published by eCommerce Strategies, Inc.
Marietta, Georgia

Surviving the Digital Jungle

Published by eCommerce Strategies, Inc.
2627 Sandy Plains Road, Suite 202
Marietta, GA 30066
(770) 565-4010
(770) 565-4062 – fax
digitaljungle@e-com.com
www.e-com.com

Second printing, revised, 2000.

ISBN: 0-9664890-3-9

Library of Congress Catalog Card Number: 99-63020

Cover Design by Bill Kopp, *www.billkopp.com*

Printed and bound in the United States of America.

Other books by Jack Shaw include: **Doing Business in the Information Age**, and **The EDI Project Planner**.

TABLE OF CONTENTS

Acknowledgements

Many people provided valuable suggestions and contributions to this book. At the risk of leaving a few unnamed, I'd like to express my appreciation for all their ideas. Thanks to each of you. And, of course, I should say that while this book is the result of the efforts of many, any omissions or errors are my responsibility alone. Among those making significant contributions are:

Chuck Stockinger, Chuck Moore, and the Board of Directors,
    American Supply & Machinery Manufacturers Association
Toby Mack, Associated Equipment Distributors
Dave Saidat, Associated Equipment Distributors
Brad Ballance, Air Transport Association
Tom DiMarco, Boeing
Michael Sandifer, Continental DataGraphics
Bob Holinski, DMR Consulting Group
James E. Hagen, Kennametal
Phil Gibson, National Semiconductor
Roger Taylor, North American Tool Corporation
Terry A. Piper, Precision Brand Products
Rick Bushnell, Quad II
Ray Reynertson, Sturtevant Richmond
Dave Oppenheim, The Cessna Aircraft Company
P.F. Atkins, 3M Industrial Markets Group

I'd also like to thank my entire family for their support, inspiration, and understanding of the time I took away from them to work on this book. Finally, I'd like to thank the staff of eCommerce Strategies for their help and support — especially Carolyn Fields and Judy Sperry. Judy particularly played a key role in this book from concept through organization, editing, production, and keeping the author on schedule.

Preface

I've been fortunate to work with eCommerce my whole career. Of course, back in 1974 when I first started in business, we didn't call it eCommerce — that term wasn't coined for another 15 years. But, we were implementing systems that involved the electronic transmission of business data between trading partners — in this case, to our banking partners. And, these systems provided millions of dollars of benefits to our business. That's eCommerce by almost anyone's definition.

I learned even then that the benefits come not from the technology itself, but from the improved business practices the technology enables. Using digital technology to enhance business practices has been a cornerstone of my career ever since.

A few years later, I found myself working for what was, at the time, the world's largest software company. I suggested we plan for incorporating electronic communications capabilities into our business management systems. Naturally, as the squeaky wheel, I was given the assignment of investigating what I soon learned was call Electronic Data Interchange or EDI.

I joined the X12 EDI Standards Committee in 1982 just before the first version of its national EDI standards was released. It was clear that adoption of EDI would require more than a well-designed set of standards. It would require a much better understanding on the part of the business community of the opportunities afforded by EDI. I took that as my mission and began speaking, writing, and consulting on the subject. By 1986, I had started my own company.

For the next eight years, I worked to help executives understand how to use EDI and related technologies, such as bar coding and work flow automation, to redesign their business processes. Business practices such as Evaluated Receipts Settlement and Vendor Managed Inventory began to reshape major industries such as automobile manufacturing and retailing. I wrote my first book, **The EDI Project Planner**, and I founded a newsletter, **EDI Executive** (later sold to a major newsletter-publishing house). I also began publishing the **Buyer's Guide to Electronic Commerce** (formerly the **Buyer's Guide to EDI**). But I was frustrated.

While EDI and its sister technologies could powerfully affect key parts of most organizations, there were still too many processes where EDI offered little added value. I knew instinctively that there must be a way to deal with these other business needs, but the technology just wasn't there yet. Then, in 1994, I first saw the World Wide Web.

It was like a bolt from the blue. I had been keeping a casual eye on the Internet since the mid-1980s. But it seemed to me (in retrospect, still fairly accurately) that the Internet was just not yet ready for prime time as a business tool. The Web changed everything. I recognized that it was exactly the tool needed to address those business processes that EDI didn't help much. Further, it could dramatically improve some other areas where the benefits of EDI were marginal.

The Web exploded onto the business world stage in the mid-1990s in a way that dwarfed the impact EDI had made when it first appeared in the mid-1980s. Nevertheless, I saw businesses making some of the same mistakes with the Web that their predecessors had made with EDI a decade earlier. Many organizations became enamored of the technology and felt putting up a web site should be their top priority whether it made any business sense or not. Others just buried their heads in the sand and hoped it would all go away before they retired.

Neither approach is a good one. For organizations that want to survive and succeed in the Digital Jungle of the 21st Century, the key is careful planning. It's not about what new technology you can slap in place in the next 90 days. It's about laying the groundwork for the changes in business practices you will make over the next two to three to five years.

My second book, *Doing Business in the Information Age: Electronic Commerce, EDI and Reengineering,* is a 400-page in-depth strategic planning and implementation manual. While it's designed to address the needs of corporate eCommerce managers, it also has an executive summary intended to help top management understand eCommerce. Thousands of companies have read and used it.

Many of the eCommerce managers who bought *Doing Business* said something else was still needed. A book designed exclusively for non-technical executives. Something that would help them appreciate the strategic implications of eCommerce and eBusiness. And something they could read in the space of a typical airplane flight.

Surviving the Digital Jungle is my response to those managers. It's designed to help you, the busy business executive, quickly and easily get up to speed on the concepts, terminology, and issues surrounding eCommerce and eBusiness. It will help you understand what your organization will need to do to implement eCommerce, and how to start the planning process.

You can wait to begin implementation while you think through your strategy. What you can't wait any longer to do is to begin the planning and education process. It starts by turning the page.

Jack Shaw
Marietta, Georgia

The Digital Jungle 1

Are you positioned to survive in the Digital Jungle? The outcomes of the transition from the industrial economy of the 20th Century to the digital economy of the 21st Century are binary. That is, you will make the transition or you will not. Halfway measures will guarantee failure. Within a few years, surviving businesses will all be eBusinesses. Those who fail to make the transition will be bought up or simply disappear.

If you plan to survive in the emerging digital economy, you need to understand what is happening in our society and in our economy, and you must recognize the implications for your business.

We have entered a new age of civilization — the Information Age. The Information Age is already proving to be as profoundly different from the Industrial Age in which most of us were born and raised as that age of airplanes and automobiles was different from the primitive agricultural eras that preceded it. *Business Week* magazine said, "Information technology affects every other industry. It boosts productivity, reduces costs, cuts inventories, facilitates electronic commerce. It is, in short, a transcendent technology — like railroads in the 19th Century and automobiles in the 20th."

In 1965, Gordon Moore, co-founder of Intel Corporation, predicted that the processing power of the computer chip would double every 18 months. For over 35 years, that prediction, known as "Moore's Law," has held true with no end in sight. Computing power is growing exponentially.

By early 1998, the first gigahertz chip had been tested in laboratories. In late 1998, IBM demonstrated the fastest computer in the world at that time - a machine capable of processing 3.9 trillion instructions per second. That's 15,000 times faster than a state of the art 1999 personal computer. It also sports over 80,000 times the memory of that same PC. However, at recent rates of advance, most people can expect to own that kind of computing power by the year 2010.

Computing power is not only growing rapidly, the cost is falling equally rapidly. The standard unit of measure for computer speed is the ability to process 1 million instructions per second (or MIPS). As recently as the late 1970s, purchasing the computing power needed to process one MIPS cost hundreds of thousands of dollars. By 1991, the cost of one MIPS computing power had dropped to $230. In 1994, it was down to $50. In 1995 it declined to $16, and by 1997, it was down to $3.42. This trend means we must plan our business models and design our business processes for a

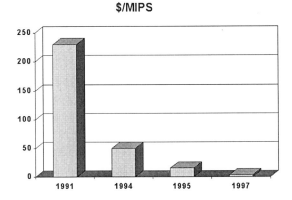

Chip Price per MIPS
$/MIPS

future where supercomputing power is virtually as free as the air we breathe and the water we drink.

Data communications capacity, or bandwidth, is also growing exponentially. The speed of dialup modems has increased from 14.4K (thousand bits per second) to 56K over the past few years. However, that is dwarfed by the arrival of cable modems and ADSL telephone lines. These new communications channels provide data communication capacities of six to 10 megabits per second. That is 100 to 500 times faster than the dialup modems of 1999.

But megabits are just a drop in the bucket compared to what is coming. At Lucent Technologies and MIT, the ability to transmit data at speeds in excess of a terabit per second has already been tested and proven. That's 1,000 gigabits or a million megabits per second. That is enough data communications capacity to download an entire three hour-long movie, uncompressed, in a fraction of a second.

Perhaps even more than hard-wired communications, wireless digital communications will impact the way we work and live.

Modem Speed — Dial Up vs. Cable/ADSL

Bits/Second (Thousands)

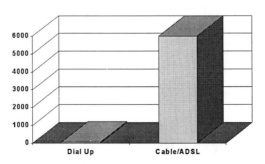

Fiber Optic Research

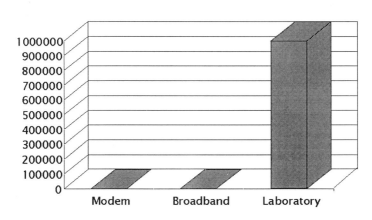

Megabits per Second

In 1998, Teledesic Corporation launched the first of its 268 satellites into low Earth orbit. When this constellation is completed, it will provide wireless, broadband, multimedia communications and computing capabilities anywhere on the planet. It will be a virtual Internet in the sky.

Try to finish the following sentence correctly: "There are more telephones in Tokyo than..." As of this writing, one answer is, "...in the entire continent of Africa." Africa may never have as many hard-wired telephones as Tokyo, but, in a few decades, it will probably have every bit as good an information technology infrastructure. Wireless digital communications will bring the Information Age to parts of the world where lack of a communications infrastructure and economic resources have held back progress over the past century. By the middle of the 21st Century, wireless digital communication will have helped to make obsolete the phrase "Third World".

The combination of the data processing and data communications explosions is bringing unprecedented capabilities to humankind. For example, we shall soon see telephone switches and other devices that provide real-time translation between people conversing in different languages. Digital highways into the home already offer instant access to the world's store of knowledge and information.

Virtual meeting rooms save people the wear and tear of air travel. Satellite-based personal communicators allow individuals to phone home from anywhere on the planet. And machines capable of emotion, inference, and learning are interacting with human beings in new ways. It appears that Star War's C3PO and Star Trek's Mr. Data may not be so far off after all!

How do you plan for the extraordinary changes taking place in our society and our economy? How do you more effectively manage your organization to ensure that it will survive such dramatic change as well as take full advantage of it?

To begin with, you must answer the question, "How will the future of our industry be different?" Specifically, you must look five years out and ask:

➢In what end product or service markets will we participate?
➢Who will our customers be?
➢How will we reach them?
➢Who will our competitors be?
➢What will our competitive advantage be?
➢Where will our margins come from?
➢What capabilities will make us unique?

To answer such questions requires more than just industry

forecasting, it requires industry foresight. The distinction is a key one. Forecasting starts with what is today and attempts to project what might happen tomorrow. Foresight starts by identifying what could be tomorrow and then determines what must happen in the interim to accomplish the desired result.

Industry foresight requires deep insight into key trends in technology, demographics, life style, and regulation in order to rewrite industry rules. Only then can you create the new competitive space that will ensure that your organization can survive and thrive in the digital economy of the 21st Century.

A study published in the *Harvard Business Review* discussed what it takes for companies to survive and succeed in the emerging digital economy. It pointed out that those companies which are most successful are those that exceed their competitors in three critical dimensions of management. Those dimensions are quality, speed, and cost.

Quality is no longer a competitive advantage, it is a competitive necessity. At leading-edge companies, the quality of their products and services is unsurpassed. In addition,

---

Three Dimensions of Management

they do things faster than the competition, whether that is filling a customer's order or bringing a new product to market. And finally, the delivered cost of their products is the lowest in the market.

Companies that excel in all three critical dimensions of management dominate their markets. Those that fall short in any one of these three critical dimensions, no matter how well they do in the other two, fall into the great majority of businesses simply struggling to survive in the market.

How can you simultaneously maximize the quality of your products and services, minimize your business process cycle times, and cut costs? The answer, at most businesses today, is that you can't do it. That is the challenge that management faces.

It is impossible to simultaneously maintain quality, reduce business process cycle times, and cut costs given today's paper-bound, people intensive business

> **eBusiness**
> — the use of digital technologies as enablers to transform business models and processes in ways not possible with traditional paper-bound communications

processes. The only way to make the changes needed to ensure that our organizations survive the transition from the industrial economy of the 20th Century to the digital economy of the 21st is to digitally transform our business models and business processes — to become eBusinesses.

eBusinesses use digital technologies as enablers to transform their business models and business processes in ways not possible with traditional paper-bound communications.

A business process is a group of related activities that produces a result of value to the customer. Process redesign is best defined in the book **Reengineering the Corporation,** by Mike Hammer and James Champy, as "the fundamental rethinking and radical redesign of businesses to achieve dramatic improvements in critical contemporary measures of performance such as costs, quality, service, and speed."

A business model represents the combination of business processes that comprise your enterprise. Typically, an enterprise business model will consist of 5-10 business processes. An eBusiness results from the total digital transformation of your business.

Transformation of business models and processes is necessary for several reasons. First, customers are demanding individualized treatment. Second, competition is getting tougher. We're in a global marketspace now, and it only takes one global competitor to raise the bar for everyone else. Third, technological change has accelerated. It's not only changing the nature of the products and services that we offer, but information technology is also increasingly being used as a strategic competitive weapon. Fourth, most organizations have fragmented processes. Our processes are built into industrial era organizational structures where stovepiped organizations allow information to flow vertically, but make it difficult for information to flow horizontally through processes that cross our traditional departmental boundaries. All this must change as we enter the 21st Century's Digital Economy.

Most of our organizations were founded in and evolved to meet the demands of the Industrial Age. Within a few short years of the onset of the Industrial Age, most of the governing monarchies in the Western world fell. History shows us that organizations designed for one age of civilization almost inevitably fail when confronted with the demands of a new era of civilization. The only exceptions are those organizations that can radically alter the way they function in order to meet new demands.

Since the early 1980s, organizations have employed a whole series of approaches and methodologies in their attempts to change how they function to meet the demands of the Information Age. As organizations mature, the approaches that they select evolve from downsizing and restructuring to continuous improvement, business process reengineering, and, ultimately, digital transformation into eBusinesses.

Three Ages of Civilization

The Agricultural Age
c. 10,000 B.C. — c. 1800 A.D.

The Industrial Age
c. 1800 A.D. — c. 1980 A.D.

The Information Age
c. 1980 A.D. — 21st Century

The Quest for Survival

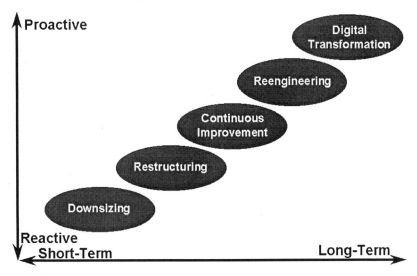

Yet some executives still ask, "Why do we need to change so fast? Can't the status quo be the way forward?" The answer is that we've entered not only a new age of civilization, but also a new economy. We are moving from the mass-market economy of the Industrial Age to the digital economy of the Information Age.

In the digital economy, information and business transaction flows have evolved from physical to virtual. We are rapidly changing from physical cash, checks, bills of lading, invoices, purchase orders, mail, phone calls, and meetings to electronic data interchange (EDI), electronic funds transfer (EFT), electronic catalogues, TV and online shopping networks, email, voice mail, and video-conferencing. The components of our economic transactions are now represented by bits of data flowing across global networks.

In some cases, the product or service that we purchase has transformed from physical to virtual. Take a look at answering machines for example. Many of us have an answering machine at home, which typically weighs a pound or two. But many of us don't have answering machines at the office. Instead we have voice mail services that we purchase from our telecommunications providers.

At the end of each year, we may spend considerably more on that virtual service than it would have cost to purchase an answering machine outright. But we don't mind spending the additional money because there are features and capabilities that can't exist in a dedicated answering machine. For example, if all the power goes down in the office and a call comes in, the voice mail service will capture the message while the answering machine can't. The voice mail service is a virtual answering machine, and a superior one at that.

The cause of our current economic change is a combination of information technology and innovation. Technology has enabled a global marketspace with ubiquitous networks of interconnected workers and consumers. This combines with the convergence in computing, communications, and content to provide unprecedented access to information.

Customers are smarter than ever before. Even products are smarter. We now have cars that know when they need to be serviced, clothes that know their size and cost, roads that know how much traffic has traveled on them, trucks that know exactly where they are located worldwide, and greeting cards that can greet the recipient in the sender's voice.

You may have received one of these recordable greeting cards. They store a spoken message of up to about 30 seconds on a chip embedded in the card. That chip contains more computing power than all the computers on planet Earth did in the year 1950. At that time there were several dozen computers around the world, each of which was as large as a basketball court. But combined, all those computers had less computing power than we casually toss into the wastebasket when we throw away one of those greeting cards.

Technology is also providing for smarter workers. Eight of ten new jobs are for knowledge workers. Technology creates a more level playing field for all competitors. This was aptly illustrated in a cartoon that appeared in *New Yorker* magazine. It shows two dogs sitting at a computer. One says to the other, "On the Internet, nobody knows you're a dog." Some may claim this refers to the tribulations of the romantically challenged in trying to use the Internet personal chat lines. Perhaps, but it's equally applicable to the idea that in the Internet's global marketspace, small businesses can compete as effectively as large ones if they're fast, flexible, and innovative. In short, as Yogi Berra once said, "The future just ain't what it used to be."

> "The future just ain't what it used to be."
> - Yogi Berra

The effects of the digital economy are being felt everywhere. No business and no industry is immune from its reach. Competition will come from sectors never before recognized as threats. What do you suppose the venerable senior management of Encyclopedia Britannica would have thought if in 1980 someone had told them that, within ten years, the very existence of their company would be threatened by computer manufacturers giving away CD-ROM encyclopedias to help sell their computers? It was competition coming from an unanticipated direction.

The tools of change that we've used in the past are no longer sufficient. Total quality management, continuous improvement, and even business process reengineering fall short in that they do not consider the enterprise as a whole. Nothing less than a carefully planned digital transformation of the enterprise can ensure its survival and success in the digital economy of the 21st Century.

Three technologies will profoundly impact our lives and our work over the next generation. These are biotechnology, molecular nanotechnology, and eCommerce. Of these three, eCommerce will undoubtedly have the most immediate effect on the way corporations and other organizations do business. By the middle of the first decade of the 21st Century, major parts of our global economy will have moved to eCommerce.

What is eCommerce? It is doing business electronically using various digital means such as the Internet, intranets, extranets, the World Wide Web, EDI, bar coding, CD- and DVD-ROMs, email, eforms, and file transfer.

To better understand the impact of eCommerce, you should ask, "How will eCommerce transform our industry?" In order to answer this question, you must first answer a series of strategic questions about eCommerce and how it will impact your industry:

➤How fast is eCommerce emerging in our industry?
➤What factors may accelerate or decelerate that emergence?
➤Who or what is driving the trend toward the use of eCommerce in our industry?
➤Who is exploiting eCommerce?
➤Which technologies are propelling eCommerce in our industry?
➤What technologies are our competitors choosing?
➤Which companies are in the lead?
➤Who has the most to gain and the most to lose?
➤How will eCommerce affect our customers' needs and demands?
➤How might it impact our business model?

➢What new product and service opportunities might eCommerce create?

➢What are our options for learning more about or influencing the use of eCommerce in our industry?

➢What happens if we fail to respond?

We will not answer all these questions in this book. Indeed, we couldn't answer these questions for you, as these are questions you must answer about your own business and industry. The best way to answer these questions is to ensure that your key executives have an in-depth understanding of the general issues involved in eCommerce. They can then comfortably, and at length, discuss and debate the answers for your company and your industry. Management should be able to agree, at least in general, on the answers that are most appropriate and effective for your organization.

> A core competency in eCommerce is a necessary prerequisite to survival and success in 21st Century business.

When your management team has acquired enough knowledge and understanding of the issues surrounding eCommerce to enable them to conduct such a discussion, your organization has achieved a core competency in eCommerce. Core competencies are skills or aptitudes that provide value to your customers; differentiate your firm from the competition; and can extend to new products, services, and markets. It's important to distinguish core competencies from endowments such as patents, brands, manufacturing capacity, distribution infrastructure, and financial assets. The key distinction is that while endowments are inherited from the past, it is core competencies that are required to move your organization into the future.

A core competency in eBusiness is a necessary prerequisite to survival and success in any industry. One objective of this book is to help you begin to understand eCommerce and eBusiness so that you can develop that core competency.

The first act toward developing a core competency is for you to determine what business your firm is in.

Let's examine Federal Express as a business entity, for example. When we initially think about Federal Express, we think of them as a package delivery business. If we're creative, we may think of them as being in the business of logistics management or customer service. But when Fred Smith, CEO of Federal Express, was asked about his business he said, "Federal Express is a world-class information management organization that happens to move parcels to pay for it." The management at Federal Express realizes that the company can't provide customer service, deliver packages, or manage logistics unless the company first manages information effectively.

Now, picture yourself working for a company that is more than 200 years old. Not simply an old company, but one that dominated its industry for that entire span of time. Imagine your shock and dismay as you watch this dominant organization dragged to its knees and the edge of bankruptcy in just 36 months by its failure to plan for the impact of eCommerce on its business.

The company is Encyclopedia Britannica, which dominated world markets for encyclopedias from the late 18th century until about 1990. At that time, previously insignificant competitors came out with encyclopedias on CD-ROMs (which allow access to any of the information in the encyclopedia in seconds, not only in text but also with graphics, sound and full-color, full-motion video). Imagine the conversation when top management at Encyclopedia

Britannica asked sales and marketing executives if this was a product line that the company ought to consider. Secure in their history and market stature, sales and marketing probably replied, "We don't need those gimmicks. Our encyclopedias are the most complete and detailed available. They're printed on the finest paper and bound with the best bindings. Plus, we have the best sales force in the encyclopedia industry. How can a flimsy piece of plastic compare?"

In just three years time, Encyclopedia Britannica's annual sales dropped from $117 million to $57 million. The company was facing the very real possibility of bankruptcy. Later we'll discuss some of the remarkable steps Encyclopedia Britannica has taken to turn the situation around. But first, let's look at the strategic error Encyclopedia Britannica made in not anticipating the impact of the CD-ROM on its business.

The situation goes beyond the fact that Encyclopedia Britannica didn't understand the technology, or even that the company didn't listen to its customers. The error was more fundamental than that — Encyclopedia Britannica didn't understand what business it was in. The company thought it was in the book business and failed to recognize that it was in the information business.

As a matter of fact, all organizations are in the information business. Studies have shown that in manufacturing companies, 70 percent of employee time and effort is spent doing knowledge work — managing information. In service organizations those percentages are even higher, sometimes approaching 100 percent. Unless we understand that we are all in the information business and unless we use the latest and most effective tools and technologies to manage our information, we may find ourselves facing the same desperate situation as Encyclopedia Britannica.

Digital Business Transformation 3

To prepare for the digital economy, companies must fundamentally rethink their core business models. They may need to rethink their missions, their products and services, their value chain, their markets and customers, their technology infrastructure, and even their organizational structures. They must be prepared not simply to modify them, but to replace any or all of them.

Digital transformation is not simply automation of existing business processes. It is not downsizing, flattening, delayering, or reorganizing. Downsizing is about doing less with less. The ultimate conclusion of downsizing is to do nothing with anyone, fire everybody, and close the doors. Digital transformation increases the productivity of your people so you can grow sales and profits faster than you need to grow the staffing levels required to maintain them.

It's also important to make a distinction between digital transformation and total quality management's concept of continuous incremental improvement. When you have an effectively designed eBusiness model supported by well-structured digital business processes, you still want to look for continuous incremental improvements to those processes. But, when you're dealing with obsolete, fragmented, paper-based business processes supporting an antiquated, Industrial Age business model, applying the concepts of continuous incremental improvement is like rearranging the deck chairs on the Titanic. It's a waste of time and resources that are better applied to rethinking your business model and the design of the process itself.

Continuous innovation should be an immediate and constant goal and should not be confused with continuous improvement. While continuous improvement makes routine small enhancements to existing business practices, products, or processes, continuous innovation requires ceaseless reevaluation of the enterprise's overall business model. You really have only two choices. You can either begin the process of transforming your business now or wait until you are forced by circumstances to start making changes — and hope you still have time.

The digital economy will differ significantly from the 20th Century's industrial economy in many important ways. It's important to understand that changes in technology move quickly. These changes will, in turn, stimulate changes in organizations, industries, and the economy as a whole.

In a fairly short span of time:

➢Multimedia supercomputers will be cheap, portable, and ubiquitous.

➢Virtually all relevant parties will be connected to the Internet.

➢All connected parties will have sufficient data communications bandwidth for effective multimedia computing and communications.

➢Appropriate security will be available. The public key infrastructure will be in place, and all parties will have secure identification. Electronic business management systems will contain strong encryption technologies.

➢National and international laws will effectively support eCommerce.

In this environment, the value-creating processes will migrate from physical assembly to knowledge creation.

18

Creativity and innovation become the critical skills for enterprise success. Unlike the factory workers of the Industrial Age, knowledge workers own the means of production. It's in their heads. The result will be that the balance of power will move from the employer to the worker. We already see this happening with such high-tech skills as Java programming. This tendency will spread throughout the economy.

The Internet, intranets, and extranets will become an integrated open platform for innovation across enterprise boundaries. This will allow smaller organizations to band together. While this open infostructure will reduce the competitive edge of large corporations, it will also facilitate the outsourcing of functions that are not within their core competencies. When we couple this move toward virtual operations with the rise of the empowered knowledge worker, what we see is that the primary role of corporations will be to become the owners of the value creating process.

We already have examples of this. For instance, a film production company owns almost none of the assets that are needed to produce a film. They hire the contractors and

---

Rethinking the Business Model

> Mission
> Organization
> Value Chain
> Products/Services
> Technology Infrastructure
> Customers
> Markets
> Not just Improve, but possibly Replace.

talent needed on a project by project basis. Their only real permanent "asset" is the set of core competencies needed to manage the value creating processes of the movie industry.

Another example is concert tours. In an interview during a recent Rolling Stones world tour, Mick Jagger accurately described himself as the chief executive officer of a $100 million virtual corporation that would go out of existence at the end of the tour.

True eBusiness doesn't take place by focusing on isolated pieces of your business. It's not enough to implement supply side integration, enhanced customer service, or improved logistics. You must develop an overall future vision of how you will do business in the digital economy.

There are two key steps in developing that vision. The first is to develop a digital industry model. You must determine what your industry will look like and how it will function in the digital economy of the early 21st Century. The second is to develop a digital business model that can most effectively leverage your company's core competencies within that digital industry environment.

To develop a digital industry model, you start with the way the industry works today. Then you put into place the driving principles of the digital economy:

Physical location becomes nearly irrelevant.

Physical assets can be sold only once, however, digital assets can be sold multiple times. Remember that even if you have a physical product, what you deliver to your customers is a combination of product, services, and information. Without the information, the value of the product is significantly reduced. That information is a digital asset, which can be leveraged much more highly than physical products or manual services.

Organizations will evolve toward the use of molecular systems, processes, and organizational structures as opposed to the Industrial Age's monolithic ones. This means that parts of businesses will become less dependent on the other parts of the same business while becoming more interdependent with the relevant parts of trading partners' businesses.

Our economy (and, indeed our society) will evolve from physical to virtual products, services, and enterprises. In effect, as the links within our organizations become looser, the boundaries between organizations also blur. The result is that, like an assembly of blocks, virtual organizations will be created out of parts of pre-existing businesses.

Therefore, in the emerging digital economy, speed, flexibility, and innovation become more important than size or assets.

An understanding of these driving principles can help to identify potential new competitors. Reasonable assumptions can be made about the evolution of information technologies as well as other technologies that may impact a given market or industry. Recognizing these evolving technologies will help to identify changing customer demands. Trends in governmental legislation and regulatory approaches may also impact products, services, and markets.

Combining the effects of changing customer demands, new competitors, evolving technologies, and governmental factors begins to provide a picture of an industry that may be very different from today's industry. We refer to the description of such an emerging industry as the digital industry model.

Following is a simple graphic example of a digital industry model. On the left side we see the traditional model of vertically integrated utilities in the electrical industry. On the right we see the results of industry deregulation and eCommerce —the digital industry model. Here we see a new player emerge, the energy trader. We also see that the same company no longer need do both energy generation and transmission, and that a third company can now handle distribution. It's a digital industry model because the relationships shown would be impractical if not impossible in a traditional paperbound environment.

Most digital industry models used for actual planning purposes will be somewhat more complex than the one shown. In general, a digital industry model consists of a diagram (or diagrams) depicting the following:

➤Each of the entities (organizations or individuals) involved in the industry at the time projected for the model

➤The flows of products and services among the various entities

➤The flows of payments among the entities

➤The flows of information among the entities

Once you've developed a vision of the future of your industry, then you're ready to develop your digital business model. The digital industry model and your company's current business model are the starting points. Considering information as a raw material, you then identify where within the information residing in and flowing through your organization you can extract value for your targeted customers and markets. The redefined value added relationships and the product, service, and information flows constitute the digital business model.

The difference between your digital business model and your current business model then drives your migration plans. It's

Digital Industry Model
Electrical Utilities

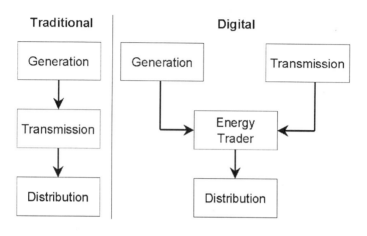

important to look several years into the future in developing your digital business model. For a small business, we must look two to three years ahead. For a larger, more complex organization, a five-to-seven year lead-time is required. This lead-time is needed to overcome the constraints inherent in your current business model. Failure to look far enough down the road can lead to incremental changes to the current business model rather than development of an effective digital business model.

In his book, **The Digital Economy**, Don Tapscott identifies three key components of value propositions in the digital economy. It's important to keep these in mind in developing your digital business model. They are content, context, and infrastructure.

Content is the products and/or services offered. Even though you may think of your business as selling specified products or services, in fact, that's not what you provide.

You deliver a package of products and services of which information is an essential part. The content is the entire package.

The second value component is context, which is where the buyer meets the seller. In other words, the context is where the exchange of value takes place.

The final value component is infrastructure, which is the set of assets and technologies needed to manage your business model.

To illustrate the concept of content, context and infrastructure, let's look at a familiar example. For a retail business such as Kmart, the content is clothing and items for the home. The context is the physical store, often located in a shopping center. The infrastructure is not only the bricks and mortar of the building, but also the display racks and cash registers. Take away any one of those three components — content, context, or infrastructure — from the industrial age business model, and you no longer have a viable business.

This scenario changes as we move into the digital economy. Content, context, and infrastructure can be unbundled. An organization can chose to participate in any one, two, or all three components for the various products and services that it provides.

With this in mind, let's review the evolution of context, content, and infrastructure by considering the changes Encyclopedia Britannica made in response to the threat of encyclopedias on CD-ROMs. It wasn't as simple as coming out with a "me too" CD-ROM product.

Encyclopedia Britannica's core competency has always been gathering, assimilating, and organizing the knowledge of the world and presenting it in a way that's understandable to the average person. That core competency hasn't changed.

Digital Economic Components

> **Content**

   The product, service, or value exchanged

> **Context**

   The meeting place for buyer and seller

> **Infrastructure**

   The technology required to enable the economic exchange

However, to compete in the emerging digital economy, Encyclopedia Britannica was forced to change the content, context, and infrastructure within which the company exercised that competency.

In its Industrial Age business model, Encyclopedia Britannica's content was knowledge of the world as printed in sets of books. Unfortunately, this knowledge began to go out of date immediately upon publication. Customers could purchase annual yearbooks to stay up with new developments, but the information in those was, of course, not integrated into the original encyclopedia. They would have to look in two (or more) books to get the whole picture.

Encyclopedia Britannica realized that to move from books that were out of date the moment they were printed to sophisticated, multimedia CD-ROMs that were out of date the moment they were created was not an effective long-term response.

Encyclopedia Britannica has changed its content to the extent that books are no longer the premier product. While the company still prints and sells books as requested, the premier product is now Britannica Online. Britannica Online is a World Wide Web site that contains the entire contents of the previously printed Encyclopedia Britannica.

Britannica Online also contains more than 700,000 hypertext links (or "hyperlinks"). These cross-reference virtually every article within Encyclopedia Britannica. In addition, they point to thousands of other web sites which hold more detailed information than is appropriate even for Encyclopedia Britannica. This new content offering now provides knowledge of the world up until the last real-time update of the database, plus the ability to automatically cross reference thousands of other information sources — a dramatic improvement over the old content model for encyclopedias.

Encyclopedia Britannica's old sales model, or context, was the use of door-to-door sales people traveling through middle- and upper-middle-class neighborhoods. These sales people talked to anxious parents trying to persuade them that if they wanted their children to go to college, they needed to buy a set of Encyclopedia Britannica books.

This sales model no longer exists. Encyclopedia Britannica has released its last door-to-door sales people. The company now sells time-dependent subscriptions. A family can subscribe to Britannica Online for less than $100 per year, and an individual student can subscribe for less than $50 per year. They also sell institutional licenses that allow colleges, universities, and similar not-for-profit organizations to subscribe at about $5 per year per student. This is a new model of pricing and delivery.

Naturally, to accommodate these changes in content and context, Encyclopedia Britannica has changed its infrastructure as well. The old infrastructure was centered around printing presses and shipping docks. Now it's about Web servers, data communications networks, and eCommerce applications.

eCommerce Technologies 4

The primary way in which eBusinesses communicate with their trading partners is through eCommerce. eCommerce can be defined as the digital transformation of those parts of your business processes that cross trading partner boundaries.

A trading partner is any person or organization outside of your own with whom you exchange information in order to conduct business. Trading partners include not only your customers, but suppliers of goods and services, employees, banks, insurance companies, healthcare providers, and governmental agencies — any person or organization with whom you exchange information on a routine basis.

Each of these trading partners is a candidate for the application of eCommerce technologies. These technologies include:

> Bar coding (and other forms of automated data capture)
> Electronic data interchange (EDI)
> CD/DVD-ROMs
> Imaging and OCR
> The Internet and EDI

Bar Coding. Bar Coding and related forms of automated data capture (such as radio frequency identification - RFI) are key to digital transformation. This is because they tie together the movement of materials and the flow of information.

Like a fax machine, bar coding can provide many of its benefits on a stand-alone basis. Unfortunately, many

Trading Partners

- ➢Customers
- ➢Suppliers of Goods
- ➢Suppliers of Services
- ➢Employees
- ➢Transportation Carriers
- ➢Banks
- ➢Insurance Companies
- ➢Health Care Providers
- ➢Governmental Agencies
- ➢Other External Information
  Sources or Recipients

---

companies evaluate bar coding only on this basis. The real benefits of bar coding come when the organization has designed processes to take full advantage of it and has integrated bar coding with other eCommerce technologies such as EDI.

Rick Bushnell says in his book *Getting Started with Bar Codes*, "Bar codes are part of your value added service for customers or even down stream distribution channels."

While bar coding is a prerequisite to digital transformation, there are also some prerequisites to bar coding. First, you must get your inventory under control. Second, you should have a clear, consistent product or part numbering scheme in place. Preferably your parts numbers will be in accord with industry or national products numbering standards such as the Uniform Product Code (UPC).

Electronic Data Interchange (EDI).   EDI is the most fundamental of eCommerce technologies. The reason lies in its definition. Electronic data interchange is the flow of information between organizations without human intervention. By eliminating unnecessary human intervention, the computer can do what computers do better than people: process routine transactions quickly and accurately 24 hours a day. This, in turn, frees up people, your most valuable resource, to do things that computers may never be able to do. That is to use their judgment, creativity, and experience to manage exceptions, solve problems, and continuously improve the business process.

In his book *Management* Peter Drucker says, "the purpose of any organization is to enable common people to do uncommon things." But if employees are using their time processing routine paperwork, you simply have common people doing common things. You must use the power of information technology to empower employees and liberate them from the routine tasks. By allowing them to use their time, talents, and energies to manage exceptions and improve the process, you will have common people doing uncommon things. Your company will not only survive, but also thrive because of it.

Bar Coding

➤ Mandatory for manufacturers, distributors, and retailers
➤ Ties physical movements to information flows
➤ Inventory MUST be under control
➤ Benefits maximized by integrating with EDI and other eCommerce technologies

EDI works by using agreed upon standards for the exchange of business information. In North America, the primary standard is ANSI X12. In Europe, it is UN/EDIFACT. These standards are compatible with one another to the point that many leading EDI software packages can handle both. The agency which coordinates these standards in the U.S. is the Data Interchange Standards Association (DISA).

EDI software translates trading partners' individual data formats into the agreed upon standards. The data is then transmitted between trading partners by an agreed upon method whether that is direct connection, third-party Value-Added Network (VAN), or the Internet.

EDI
— the flow of information between organizations *without human intervention*

EDI is unique among eCommerce technologies in that it allows for the exchange of data between trading partners without any human intervention required at either end. Other eCommerce technologies, including email and the World Wide Web, require human intervention at one or both trading partners' locations for the exchange of even the most routine information.

Almost any type of business information can be exchanged via EDI. More than 300 different EDI transactions have already been defined or are in use in various industries around the U.S. and around the world. Some of the most commonly used EDI transactions are those used in the sale and purchase of tangible products, e.g., requests for quote, quote, PO acknowledgment, order status, invoice, ship notice, and even payment with remittance advice. Electronic funds transfer (EFT) is simply a specialized form of EDI.

In my earlier book, *Doing Business in the Information Age*, I stated, "Traditional EDI implementations usually focus on the needs of a specific business process, often at the request of an important trading partner to exchange a specific, single document. ...(In these cases,) Business management systems remain virtually unchanged as EDI is merely adapted to the existing system."

You can actually go through your company's entire procurement cycle, or sales cycle, and replace all of the information that is exchanged verbally or on paper with EDI transactions. But, if that's all you do, it doesn't gain you much. You will have taken yesterday's Industrial Age, paper-bound business processes and simply cast an electronic shell around them. That's not the objective. The objective is not just to use the tools, but to use them to digitally transform your business and processes and achieve sustainable strategic advantages as you move ahead.

Flow of EDI Information

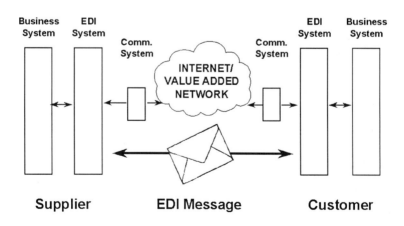

Commonly Used EDI Messages

Supplier   **Customer**

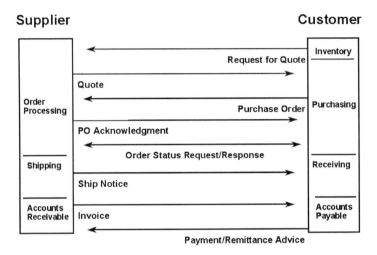

Payment/Remittance Advice

Imaging and Optical Character Recognition (OCR).
Why not scan all your documents, instead of using EDI, and
then disseminate the images to the relevant departments in
your organization?

There are two times when imaging makes sense. The first is
when you actually need an image—that is, a picture. The
second is for data capture on an interim basis only.

If you need to convey the physical appearance of such things
as a person's face, a product, the scene of an accident, an
injury, or a home for sale, nothing short of an image will
suffice. Incorporating such visual data into your databases
and communications makes excellent sense. In fact, as
bandwidth increases, it becomes highly desirable.

Imaging is the two-sided coin of eBusiness technologies. It's
often highly touted as an instant solution to paperwork.
There is no doubt that imaging is a powerful technology,

and, if applied correctly, can yield very effective results. But it's often misused.

Keep in mind that the objective is to capture the transaction data, not just a picture of the piece of paper the data is on. Images require human intervention for conversion to digital form. Optical Character Recognition (OCR) can help to convert images to digital form, but it has two significant limitations.

First, at best, OCR achieves 98%–99% accuracy. Second, even if the character can be read accurately, paper documents lack a consistent layout. So, for example, a given string of characters could be a part number, a quantity, or a ZIP code. People must still review the results even if the data doesn't have to be rekeyed.

Imaging documents does have value as an interim technology. That is, you may want to scan certain paper documents while your trading partners are getting up to speed with EDI or Web-based transactions.

Tools such as Web-to-EDI translators can be used to convert virtually all trading partners to eCommerce within a year or two. Imaging may be justified for infrequent or first time trading partners, but the scale of the implementation is vastly different from one that assumes most or all transactions will continue to come in on paper indefinitely.

The bottom line on imaging is this: Use it wherever you actually need images. Minimize or avoid its use altogether if the purpose is primarily to capture data. Instead, use EDI or Web-based commerce to capture that data in digital form from the beginning.

CD/DVD-ROMs. CD-ROMs may have an important role to play in digitally transforming business, but be aware that

CD-ROMs are an interim technology. Evenutally, the Web will replace them. DVD-ROMs are a new form of CD-ROM with 8-30 times the storage capacity of traditional CD-ROMs. DVD-ROMs can move data into memory at more than a megabit per second. While this is much faster than even a 56k-dialup connection, it is much slower than a cable modem or an ADSL line.

Within the next few years, CD-ROMs and even DVD-ROMs will be phased out in favor of the Web. The key question then becomes, "Can we gain enough strategic benefit in the meantime to justify not only the cost of implementing CD-ROMs, but the diversion of key resources to CD-ROM's from other, perhaps more deserving, eCommerce technologies?" If not, then perhaps CD-ROMs aren't appropriate for your organization.

The Internet and EDI. The Internet is changing the underlying paradigm of sales and purchasing. Buyers now refuse to thumb through outdated catalogues and leave voice mail messages with suppliers. They want to browse the World Wide Web and examine a product in detail, from all angles. They want to watch a video demonstration of a service being rendered or download a full-blown 3-D virtual reality simulation of a product in use. Buyers can then make their purchasing decisions, securely enter the purchase order number or credit card number, place the order, and follow up on it electronically.

We have learned over the years that one technology does not necessarily displace another technology. It builds upon the previous technologies. So the Internet will not replace all of the technologies we've discussed, but instead will build upon them. The Internet is a great way to find a new source for products and services. When you find a product or service you like, you will want to continue doing business with the provider. But, will you want to log on to the Internet each time to do so?

Suppose a buyer finds a supplier offering needed products on the World Wide Web. The buyer may decide to establish an ongoing relationship with that supplier. If there is an automated purchasing system, a human being will not have to log on to the World Wide Web and fill out an order for every routine repurchase of the specified products. Instead, an automated inventory system can detect a reorder point and calculate an order quantity. The inventory system would generate a requisition and pass it into the purchasing system which, in turn, would create an electronic purchase order and transmit it to the supplier via EDI.

This frees up the buyer to spend valuable time and attention on finding sources of supply for new products and services that may be required or finding new sources of supply, if necessary, for existing products or services.

EDI is already being exchanged over the Internet. The security issues and the ability to interoperate have already been addressed. This means that, once you have the software which allows you to send and receive EDI messages over the Internet, you can do so with any other organization capable of Internet-based EDI without having to worry about whether your software is compatible.

The open issue with EDI over the Internet is speed and reliability. Most of the Internet is high speed and highly reliable; however, there are a few corners where transmissions may be delayed or inappropriately routed. Of course, this is possible for private VANs also, but much less likely. This means that certain types of EDI transmissions are still not appropriate for the Internet.

Envision the following common scenario: You have a customer nearby who uses your parts in their assembly. You both agree that to control the receiving process accurately, they will not receive parts from you without an advance Ship Notice. However, because they are using just-in-time inventory, if your parts do not arrive within 15 minutes of the scheduled arrival time, the customer may have to shut down their assembly line. In this case, you probably don't want to transmit Ship Notices through the slower public Internet. It would make more sense to pay a premium to send them via a private network, which may guarantee delivery within, say, five minutes. This is similar to using an overnight delivery service for a time-critical package.

At the same time, most business information exchanges are NOT both mission critical and time critical. For these kinds of transactions (for example, invoices), there is no purpose served to pay a premium to get the information there in 5 minutes.

Two new EDI capabilities are playing an increasing role in fulfilling the promise of universal EDI with one's trading partners.

Web-to-EDI translators (often referred to as Web-based EDI or Web-EDI) allow a smaller or less sophisticated trading partner to enter information on a Web form that is translated into an EDI transmission upon submission. This way small customers can send their orders via EDI without implementing full-blown EDI translators, and small suppliers can send invoices the same way. All they need is a Web browser.

Similarly, EDI-to-Web translators allow hub companies to send out their transmissions via EDI to Web sites where they are translated into Web "pages" that the receivers can access and download or print out. This technology does not provide the less sophisticated trading partners with the full benefits of integrated EDI, but it does allow both hub and spoke to communicate electronically much more easily than in the past.

A small customer might log onto a supplier's Web site and fill out an order form that is transmitted via EDI to the supplier's customer order management system. Later, the customer receives an email linking to the supplier's Web site to download an invoice for the product. Web-based EDI has tremendous potential to eliminate paperwork. For example, at The Cessna Aircraft Company, more than 1,000 suppliers implemented Web-based EDI in less than six months.

Some ask, "Why not just have the Web site directly integrated into the business management systems and skip the EDI step?" In some cases, where real time data is both required and available, and where security can be properly managed, this is the right way to go. But in many other cases, especially if there is a legacy EDI implementation already in place, Web-EDI can be more beneficial.

The bottom line is that EDI will be with us for many years. It will leverage the Internet in many ways, and it will continue to be an important, powerful, and effective business tool.

Integrating Digital Technologies

5

In his book **Cybercorp**, James Martin describes the emerging cybercorporation of the 21st Century as a sense and respond organism that monitors its environment continuously for threats and opportunities and responds to those instantaneously and organically like a wild carnivore. When a lion is stalking through the savannah, and it smells prey or senses the hunter, it doesn't stop to call a committee meeting. It reacts immediately to the threat or opportunity. Those businesses that survive the transition to the digital economy will do the same.

To survive, companies must combine electronic commerce technologies with internal digital technologies to enable the transformation of their business models and business processes — to become an eBusiness. These paperless technologies include:

> ➢ Rules-based business management systems
> ➢ Network computing
> ➢ Electronic messaging
> ➢ Workflow automation
> ➢ Digital signatures

Rules-based business management systems. Many companies use EDI today with automated business management systems, but because of how they use it, the benefits are minimal. In such cases, information enters the organization electronically and is passed into an EDI translation software package often sitting on a stand-alone PC. It is then translated and printed out so it can be re-keyed into the appropriate business management system. This is a

Low Level EC Integration

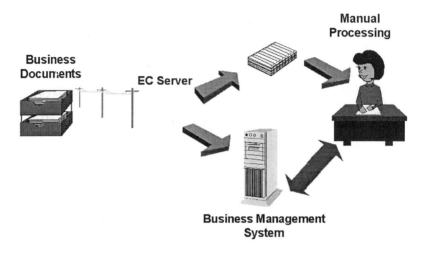

complex and expensive way of setting up the equivalent of a fax machine.

Fortunately, many companies have recognized the inherent absurdity of this process and have written interfaces to their automated business management systems so that information can be sent directly into those systems. Unfortunately, all too often that information is spit right back out again. The reason is that most of our legacy systems were not designed with eCommerce in mind. They were designed simply to record the results of the decisions made by people outside of the system and not to be able to make those decisions themselves.

Data processing without decision-making was the right structure for software until the mid-1980s when suddenly EDI came along and yanked the rug out from under that key assumption. With EDI, information can go directly into business management systems. Leading-edge companies are building rules-based, decision-making capabilities into their business management software systems. The data that enters via EDI or other forms of eCommerce can be processed immediately by those systems without human intervention so long as everything matches up with expectations.

Further, companies can define limits for common exceptions and allow the systems to manage those exceptions electronically so long as all the incoming data falls within defined limits. For example, if you have an open invoice from a customer for $10,000 and you get a check for $9,999, you aren't going to waste time, effort, and customer goodwill chasing down that $1.00 discrepancy. You're just going to write it off.

But do we have to have a human being involved in the process? An automated accounts receivable system can handle the transaction without human intervention so long as that discrepancy falls within limits defined by management. Whether that limit is $5.00, $10.00, or $100.00 is up to management.

Technically speaking, it's an exception. But it's an exception that can be managed by the system. Only when data falls outside of those management-defined limits does it then become necessary for humans to intervene in the process. Even then, exceptions can be handled electronically, which we will discuss later.

Some organizations are combining the use of EDI and rules-based functionality into integrated business management systems. In a wide variety of industries, the use of evaluated receipt settlement (ERS) or invoiceless payments is increasing. With ERS, the customer uses EDI to transmit a purchase order to the supplier. Traveling via EDI means that the purchase order moves from the customer's purchasing system to the supplier's order management system without human intervention in a matter of hours if not minutes. The data pertaining to what is being purchased; including the price, quantity, and terms of sale; is completely synchronized in both companies' automated systems.

When it's time for the supplier to ship the product, an electronic ship notice is transmitted telling the customer the quantities of the items being shipped. As soon as the customer's system can confirm receipt of that shipment, it automatically matches that ship notice quantity to the purchase order price. It then creates an obligation and posts it into the cash disbursement system for payment at the appropriate date according to the terms of sale on the purchase order.

In this scenario, the old paper invoice is not simply restructured to fit an EDI format and then transmitted electronically. The need for the concept of the invoice as a business document has been eliminated altogether, along with the need for human intervention. The process itself has been redesigned.

Evaluated Receipts Settlement

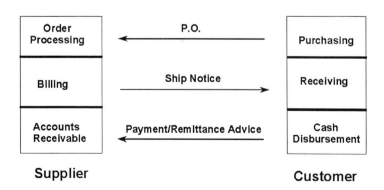

Order Processing	← P.O. ———————	Purchasing
Billing	Ship Notice ——————→	Receiving
Accounts Receivable	← Payment/Remittance Advice ———	Cash Disbursement

Supplier   **Customer**

Many companies in the retail industry have gone beyond simply eliminating the invoice. They've redefined their business model to eliminate purchase orders. Leading mass merchandisers like Wal-Mart, Kmart, JC Penney, and Target now send key suppliers daily point-of-sale data, usage data, and consumption data rather than traditional orders. These companies give their suppliers a starting inventory level, and the supplier determines how much the company has left on hand at any given point. The supplier then uses detailed daily sales or consumption data to anticipate the required demand and determine whether the customer is going to need more, how much, and when.

The customers provide very powerful incentives to the suppliers to maintain optimal inventory levels. Wal-Mart uses one of the most effective techniques. Wal-Mart tells its key suppliers that along with daily usage data, they will receive an electronic funds transfer for the value of product that has been sold on that day. If the supplier's business model processes and systems cannot handle the quick response and flexibility this requires, then they either don't

Continuous Replenishment

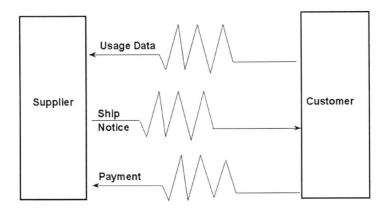

do business with Wal-Mart or they supply 60-90 days worth of product and then wait until it is all sold to get paid.

Pennzoil Motor Oil increased sales to mass merchandise channels of distribution by 16 percent in just six months. This is a significant increase for a mature product moving through an established distribution channel. At the same time, it increased inventory turns of its product at retail to 99 times a year.

Pennzoil, as a major supplier to Wal-Mart, uses that detailed daily sales data combined with their knowledge of the demographics of motor oil consumption to keep inventory levels at Wal-Mart down to a four days' supply. Now Wal-Mart pays in five days. How can Wal-Mart possibly justify paying in five days' time for products on which the company used to have 30-day terms? It's easy. Wal-Mart now has negative working capital invested in inventory. The company doesn't have to pay for the oil until after it has already been sold. Meanwhile, Wal-Mart's customers are finding the right size can of motor oil on the shelf more often. This is why sales rose 16 percent in six months. It's a win-win-win scenario.

Skeptics might ask, "How can everyone win? Don't we have to have a loser here somewhere?" No. Business does not have to be a zero sum game. In this case, we have substituted information for inventory. Of course, eCommerce isn't going to give you 100 percent perfect foresight. But the problem isn't that companies don't achieve 100 percent foresight. The problem is that they don't even have 100 percent knowledge of what happened yesterday.

Complete knowledge about what happened yesterday, however, is now possible. Business models with processes and systems that give information in real-time are a reality. Information at a level of detail and in an electronic machine processable form that allows you to perform analysis and projections is also a reality. Even though you can never achieve 100 percent forecasting capabilities, you can dramatically improve your forecasting and subsequently reduce inventories and take cost out of the system as a whole.

Since the late 1980s, textile manufacturers, apparel manufacturers, and apparel retailers in the U.S. have jointly taken more than $25 billion worth of inventory out of the supply chain. They have reduced the average turnaround for new apparel items to be delivered to retail stores from six months to six weeks. This turnaround has proved beneficial for the U.S. apparel manufacturing industry. Since the early 1970s, U.S. retail stores had sold a larger percentage of apparel items manufactured outside the U.S. than those manufactured domestically. In the early 1990s, that trend changed and now the percentage of apparel goods made in the U.S. for U.S. markets has increased each year for the past five years.

Network computing. If you want to eliminate paperwork and move to paperless electronic processes, you need to go beyond EDI alone and incorporate network computing into your business. Tying together the network of your company is an important component.

In the ideal company scenario, every person with a desk and a telephone has a dedicated workstation. Employees can not only communicate with every other person in the company, but they also can access every automated business management system in the company, subject to appropriate security controls. Every system and every person can exchange information electronically at light speed regardless of where they are geographically located.

If this scenario doesn't describe how your firm works today, it describes how it must operate soon. The management of those companies likely to survive the transition to the Digital

Economy recognize that this is where their business must be within the next few years.

Electronic Messaging. Another tool needed for paperless processes is electronic messaging, which is the exchange of electronic objects between a source and a target. Sources and targets are intelligent business entities that generate and/or process business information.

There are two major types of sources and targets, a person or a rules-based business management system.

Electronic objects are digitized files of business information. All business information falls into one of six categories — unstructured text, structured data, graphics, image, voice, or video.

If you are using electronic messaging technology to exchange unstructured text messages between people, this is referred to as interpersonal messaging, but more commonly called email. Using the same technology to exchange structured data files between automated business management systems without human intervention is called EDI. Many companies overlook the possibility of using internal EDI across their corporate wide area network as an enabler to redesign their business processes.

Workflow Automation. Workflow automation is the exchange of structured data between people and automated business management systems. It's through workflow automation that we allow for human intervention in paperless processes.

An example of workflow automation is the best way to describe this technology. Suppose we've decided to remodel a remote office. We've contracted with a local construction company, and part of the deal is that the company receives a

30 percent progress payment. In a paper-based environment, we send a paper purchase order to the contractor. The contractor renders services to us, but we have no receiver for construction services as we might have for some tangible commodity product.

When the contractor mails an invoice to the accounts payable department, the department has no receiver with which to match it. The department then pulls the contract to find out what is needed for approvals against this purchase order. The document states that the department needs signatures from Mary in the engineering department and Joe at the local site in field operations. The accounts payable department sends the request for payment first to Mary and then to Joe through company mail.

When the payment request gets back to the accounts payable department weeks later, the department processes it for payment. If the terms are 2 percent 10, net 30, it is too late to take the discount because of the length of the

---

Traditional A/P—Purchase of Services (Paper-Based)

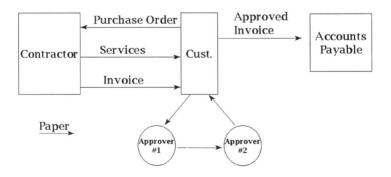

approval process. Lost discounts are just one of the problems we may have when we process paper documents through our organizations.

Let's put EDI and a rules-based business management system into this scenario. The purchase order can be sent electronically and the invoice can be submitted electronically. Here's where workflow automation comes in, and this is what leading edge companies are doing today. When the electronic invoice comes into the rules-based accounts payable (AP) system, the system determines that the invoice is for services. It then sends an electronic query about necessary approvals across the corporate wide area network to the purchasing system, which could be on a computer in a different building or even on a different continent.

Within a few seconds to a few minutes, depending on how busy the network and the systems are, the AP system receives a response from the purchasing system that signatures are required from Mary and Joe. The AP system formulates a request to obtain signatures of approval or rejection from both Mary and Joe and then passes that to the EFRA (electronic forms routing and approval) system. The EFRA system is workflow automation software that resides on the corporate wide area network and keeps track of all the electronic forms moving through the organization.

An original paper document can be in only one place at a time, but electronic forms can be multiple places at the same time. The purchase order can be simultaneously routed to both Mary and Joe, or a link to the internal URL where the invoice can be found on the corporate intranet can be emailed to both.

When Mary comes in from lunch, she checks her workstation and sees her email icon flashing. She sees it is a message from the accounts payable system that she needs to

EDI & Work Flow Automation (Electronic)

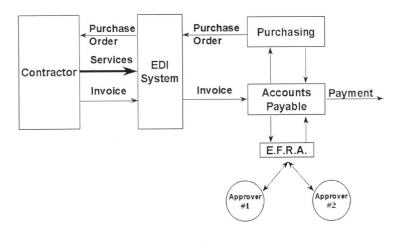

review this particular invoice for approval. Well aware of the status of the project, she enters her approval, applies her digital signature, and forwards that electronic form back to the EFRA system. Once the EFRA system has received responses from both Mary and Joe, it passes them to the accounts payable system, which validates the signatures as approvals. The system then sets up the invoice for payment at the appropriate date according to the terms of sale on the purchase order.

We haven't completely eliminated human intervention from the process, but we don't want to. This is exactly the kind of exception situation where we need human experience and the judgment factor to come into play. What we have done is eliminate the paperwork, errors, delays, and impact on people's productivity required to manage that exception in a traditional paper-based business environment.

Whether it's travel expenses, requisition approvals, order pricing, claims adjudication, or even concurrent engineering, companies are integrating workflow automation into their redesigned digital business processes.

Digital signatures. In the workflow automation scenario, Mary used a digital signature to approve the invoice. Many of us use digital signatures on a regular basis without even realizing it. Every time you go to a cash machine, you are using a digital signature. It consists of the combination of the data on the magnetic stripe on the back of your ATM card plus your PIN.

When thinking of digital signatures, many people envision what their handwritten signatures would look like if they were displayed on a computer screen. While there are devices that will capture an image of your handwritten signature electronically, these suffer from the same shortcomings that handwritten signatures on pieces of paper have had for centuries. That is, the signatures are relatively easy to forge and difficult to verify.

Through public key encryption, Mary easily can identify herself uniquely. Mary's private key can be stored on a device such as a smart card or even a computer ring and released through voiceprint or fingerprint identification. Any person or system to which Mary wants to confirm her signature will be given Mary's public key.

Using these tools, businesses can design systems to authenticate signatures, verify that documents have not been altered, encrypt documents to hide them from prying eyes and provide for non-repudiation. Non-repudiation means that the sender of the document cannot disclaim having sent it nor can the receiver of the document deny having received it.

The primary question is this: In a properly designed digital business environment, is our security as good, is our audit trail as clear, and is the legal basis for our business transactions as sound as in the traditional paper and ink environment? The answer is, "No!"

If your digital business environment is designed correctly: Your security will be far stronger, your audit trails will be more complete and accurate, and, ultimately, the legal basis for your business transactions will be more sound than they ever were in your traditional paper-based environment.

The Internet Impact   6

Business Week magazine stated that the Internet would change the way we do business more than the invention of the computer did. *The Economist* went even farther saying that it would change the way we work, and the way we live, more than the invention of the telephone — more than the invention of television. In fact, they said it was quite simply the most important invention in the last 500 years — exceeded in all the history of human kind only by the inventions of the wheel and the printing press.

Traffic on the Internet is doubling every 100 days. At the beginning of 1997, 40 million people worldwide had access to the Internet. By 2000, that had increased to 200 million people around the globe. It is estimated that two-thirds of U.S. homes will be online by the year 2003. Experts estimate that by the year 2005, over one billion people worldwide will have access to the Internet.

The World Wide Web is already the fastest growing technology in history. It took radio 38 years to reach 50 million people. Television reached 50 million people in 13 years from the time it became commercially available. The World Wide Web reached 50 million people in just four years.

Online air travel sales, just $200 million in 1996, quadrupled to $800 million in 1997, nearly tripled again in 1998 to over $2 billion, and reached $5 billion in the year 2000.

Time to Reach 50,000,000 People

(Years)

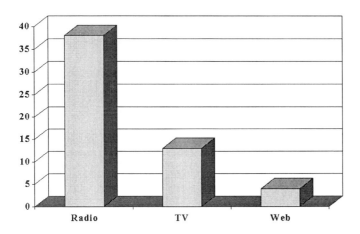

By the year 2005, Internet Commerce could account for more than half of the gross domestic product of the U.S. In fact, by that time, some retailing experts predict the number of retail stores in the United States will be reduced by 25% to 50%. This is not because they expect a massive depression, but rather because many retail outlets will simply no longer be needed. They'll have become superfluous in an era of online commerce.

Many companies using Internet Commerce have shown explosive growth. They include:

Autobytel. Autobytel sells automobiles over the Internet. In just two years they went from $1.8 billion in cars sold to over $6 billion.

Amazon.com. Amazon.com is the leading seller of books on the Internet. In 1996, Amazon's first full year of online operations, it sold $16 million in books or an average of

$4 million per quarter. In 1997, Amazon sold $148 million in books or $37 million per quarter. In 1998, 4th Quarter sales <u>alone</u> topped $250 million!

Dell. In the first quarter of 1997, Dell computers sold $1 million per day in computers via the World Wide Web. In the second quarter that figure increased to $2 million per day. In the third quarter it was $3 million per day, and by early 1998 Dell was selling over $5 million worth in computers on line every day. In early 1999, Dell was selling over $14 million worth in computers online *every day*. At that point, Dell was generating 25 percent of its revenue from online sales. By the end of 2000, Dell expects to hit 50 percent.

Cisco. Cisco is a leading manufacturer of data communications routers. (Routers are the networking hardware that switches, or routes, data communication traffic from one point to another on the Internet or on other networks.) In 1996, when Cisco began selling their routers online, they sold $10 million in routers online per month. In

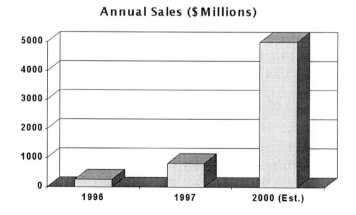

Online Air Travel Sales

Annual Sales ($Millions)

Internet Sales Growth—Dell

Daily Sales ($Millions)

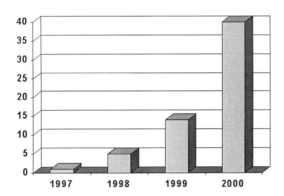

1997, that figure escalated to $125 million and in 1998, Cisco sold $350 million per month via the World Wide Web. By 1999, Cisco generated over 80% of its sales online — over half a billion dollars in online revenues per month.

Overall, according to Forrester Research, business-to-business commerce via the Internet increased dramatically from just $600 million in 1996 to $100 billion in 1999 to a projected $1.3 trillion in 2003! At that point Internet Commerce will account for 9 percent of U.S. business trade. A study completed by the University of Texas in 1999 showed that 1998 Internet Commerce sales were actually $102 billion, more than two and one-half times Forrester's estimate. It is possible we may see Internet Commerce sales hit the one trillion dollar mark by 2001.

Strategic Web Site Design Issues. The top business Web sites have several key characteristics in common according to *Business Marketing* magazine. Each year it lists the

NetMarketing 200, a compilation of top business-to-business Web sites. Results show that, of the top sites:

➤66% take orders and payments online
➤76% recruit employees online
➤86% distribute product online (for example, software)
➤96% provide online customer care

The 66% figure is both the most important and the most misleading. The top 200 business Web sites grossly over-represent the proportion of business sites that actually allow customers to place orders and remit payments online. At the same time, as we move into the Digital Economy, the ability to place orders and remit payments online will become practically universal.

Online recruitment today is fairly simplistic. Most sites merely provide contact information and, in a few cases, allow for submission of applications. Again, as we move into the digital economy, recruitment will become much more sophisticated. For example, we'll see online skills testing and personality assessment. This will let a candidate know how well he or she meets the prospective employer's profile of successful employees before they even submit an application.

The 86% of top business Web sites that distribute product online is a near term anomaly. It reflects the exceptional number of information technology companies among the initial top Web site operators. As the mainstream of the global economy goes digital, more and more of the top business Web sites will be those offering tangible products that can't be digitized. So, in fact, the decline we'll see in this number over the next few years will reflect the maturation of the digital economy.

Finally, the fact that 96% of the top Web sites provide online customer care is most revealing. In short, you can't be one of the best unless you provide top-notch customer care. Powerful, effective online customer care will continue to be mandatory for business Web sites.

Well-designed Web sites have several additional elements in common. Jakob Nielsen of Useit.com recommends the following:

Be leading edge not bleeding edge. This means you should use current, mature and widely available technology in your site. You don't want it to be technologically out of date, but there are two good reasons not to implement every untried new technology in the market. First, new technologies tend to be unreliable. Second, even if it works, trading partners around the world who access your web site may not have the necessary plug-ins or other software needed to use your new technology.

Weed out old information. One of my consulting clients had a page on their site titled, "New Product Developments." The latest entry was dated May 1996. My question was whether they hadn't developed any new products since 1996, or whether they just didn't care if Web site visitors knew about them. There's no shortcut. Keep your Web site up to date. No information that can be dated should be more than a month old.

Minimize download times. This almost goes without saying, but too many sites still require visitors to sit through interminable downloads of large graphics or large numbers of graphics. If your Web site will be designed through an internal network or from a T-1 line, be sure to test all the downloads through a connection no faster than 28k. It will give you a very different perspective on your site.

Simplify your URLs. Your Uniform Resource Locator (URL) is the web "address" that visitors key in to access your web site. Keep them as clear and simple as possible. For example, www.ecommercebookstore.cc is reasonably self-explanatory. This not only helps visitors to understand the design of your site, it also helps them to remember the URL.

Intranets. Intranets are internal "Web sites" that are accessible only to those within an organization. They use the same Internet Protocols (IP) as the public Internet, so that people can use their Web browsers to access and process internal information. By making corporate information readily available online, companies can speed up business processes and share information much more effectively.

Some of the most effective uses of Intranets are in human resources. Companies are putting online their travel guidelines, expense forms, employee handbooks, employee directories, current financials, employee newsletters, internal surveys, and even the company cafeteria menu. Other companies are conducting internal recruiting on their intranet, providing job aids and reference materials, and using the intranet for notification of and registration for classroom and conference training.

In product development and manufacturing, companies are using intranets to help their people collaborate on design issues. Online chat groups or discussion rooms help interdisciplinary and geographically decentralized product teams share ideas. Design guides, engineering reference manuals, and related materials are accessible online. Some companies publish their engineering project information online: schedules, action plans, progress reports, product specifications, design ideas, and team member contact information.

Others publish a Frequently Asked Questions (FAQ) list for the best product development practices and procedures. Still others put all their process documentation online: quality assurance documentation such as ISO9000 documentation, CAD drawings, design standards, technical information, and cost information.

Extranets. Extranets are intranets, or parts of intranets, for which organizations provide secure access to specified trading partners. Extranets are used for a variety of business processes.

Procurement is an area ripe for digital transformation and the tools are rapidly becoming available to do it. Many businesses are integrating EDI with rules-based inventory systems and implementing continuous replenishment with their key suppliers in order to optimize raw material and parts procurement. By receiving either consumption data or production scheduling information, suppliers are able to ensure a logistically optimal flow of parts and materials.

It appeared that Materials, Repair, and Operating supplies (MRO) procurement was immune to the benefits of digital technology until the arrival of Web-based procurement. Now purchase of MRO items, as well as office supplies and services is fast becoming paperless. Online catalog systems are reducing training costs and effort, providing centralized controls for decentralized purchasing, and enabling "best practices" and new purchasing strategies. By aggregating purchasing with controlled sourcing, these systems provide standardized purchase sourcing, increase internal purchase leveraging, control purchasing "leakage", and reduce inventory levels.

In Web-based procurement systems, suppliers place their catalogs on a secure extranet where they can update product, pricing, and inventory availability information. Requisitioners and buyers within an organization then access these supplier catalogs through a standard interface on their corporate intranet using their Web browsers. These interfaces provide easy, logical searches across all supplier catalogs making it easy to find the best prices and terms.

The better systems provide private pricing information for customers. This means that if a supplier is offering items at below list price, the supplier can make those prices available to a specific customer on their extranet without competitors on the same customer's extranet being able to see the discounts offered.

Organizations can choose among three alternative approaches to implementing Web-based procurement:

The first is the simplest and cheapest in that organizations simply access eCatalogs on individual suppliers' Web sites for ordering. In some cases, if the relationship is significant enough to the supplier, the customer may be able to access a secure extranet. There they may find customized pricing, packaging, and/or product availability.

This approach, while least taxing to customer resources also provides the most superficial benefits. It's inconvenient to compare prices and availability across multiple suppliers and appropriate entries must be entered into internal procurement systems.

The second is the most difficult and expensive approach to implement. The customer arranges for all their key suppliers to maintain eCatalogs with up-to-date pricing and availability on the customer's intranet. This approach requires the suppliers to transmit daily updates of pricing and availability (typically using EDI). This means that the customer must have pretty strong leverage with their suppliers.

Additionally, the customer must maintain updates in a database accessible through their Intranet. For smaller businesses, this can be technologically daunting. There are software packages designed to support in-house supplier eCatalogs; however, they are very expensive.

The primary benefit of this approach for the few large companies that can use it, is that it ensures that all the company's key suppliers are available through a single centralized Web-based procurement system. These systems also make it very easy to quickly compare pricing and availability across all the relevant suppliers.

The third approach takes a middle road. Certain third-party service providers offer secure Web sites which host the eCatalogs of many suppliers of the kinds of MRO items typically purchased online. Customers can access these sites, compare pricing and availability, and purchase products. For additional fees, some of these providers will integrate the purchasing information back into the customer's legacy procurement system.

This approach tends to be somewhat less expensive than hosting eCatalogs on the customer site though considerably more expensive than accessing separate eCatalogs hosted on supplier sites. At the same time, this third-party approach provides more functionality than supplier hosted eCatalogs. Perhaps the biggest drawback to this approach is getting all of the customer's key suppliers to join and update the same third-party site.

As technologies such as eXtensible Markup Language (XML) (which will be discussed more later in this chapter) mature, Web-based procurement will be simplified. Browsers will be able to access multiple sites simultaneously, comparing pricing and availability of a given product across eCatalogs. Sophisticated suppliers will host their own XML-capable eCatalogs. Smaller or less sophisticated suppliers will likely continue to use the service of third-party providers. In the meantime, companies wishing to conduct Web-based procurement must choose among the three alternatives currently available.

Electronic Payments. The payment process is also becoming easier to manage electronically. For 10 years or so, financial EDI has enabled companies to manage incoming and outgoing payments electronically. While its use has grown steadily, it has always required the up front implementation effort of any EDI transaction. Now, the combination of corporate purchasing cards and Web-based procurement is making electronic payments for ad hoc purchases practical and profitable.

Prior to 1998, the great concern limiting payments over the Internet was security. While credit card information submitted to secure web sites was far safer than handing your credit card to a waiter in a restaurant, the perception that fraud was rampant on the Internet still caused problems. With the introduction by VISA, MasterCard, and other major credit card companies of the Secure Electronic Transactions (SET) protocol, concerns about Internet fraud are greatly reduced.

With SET, a Certificate Authority issues a digital certificate to the cardholder. This is an electronic token attesting that the cardholder is, in fact, the legally responsible party for purchases made with this card.

Using Public Key Encryption the certificate confirms the cardholder's digital signature for purchases made using the card. It is issued at the time the card is issued or updated. It will typically be stored either in an electronic wallet on the cardholder's PC or handheld computer or it may be stored on a smart card or computer ring.

The steps in secure electronic transactions are (see diagram which follows):

1. Initiate Purchase
The cardholder transmits authorization to charge their account in exchange for goods or services purchased. Unlike telephone credit card sales or most initial online credit card charges, with SET the credit card number is encrypted and the merchant never sees the cardholder's actual credit card number.

2. Authorization Request

The merchant's software adds the merchant's identification and the transaction amount to the cardholder's encrypted account information and transmits it to the credit card processor. If the merchant's account is with a large bank, the bank may process the charge. If not, the charge will likely be forwarded to one of the major third-party credit card processors for handling. The card processor has the public key for cardholders in order to decrypt the credit card data and pass the authorization request to the cardholder's bank for approval.

3. Cardholder Authorization

The cardholder's bank responds to the card processor with either an approval or denial of credit. The card processor then passes that information along to the merchant. If credit is denied, the merchant informs the customer.

Secure Electronic Transactions

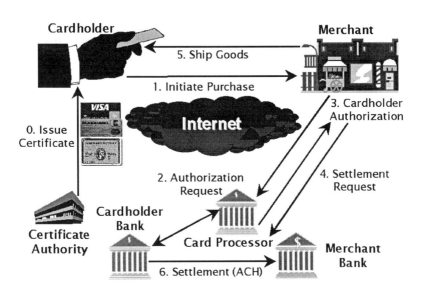

4. *Settlement Request*

If credit is approved, the merchant sends a request to the card processor to remit funds to the merchant's account. The request is passed along to the cardholder's bank.

5. *Ship Goods*

The merchant ships the goods or performs the service according to the cardholder's instructions.

6. *Settlement*

The cardholder's bank transfers funds to the merchant's bank via a private credit card clearing system. This is the only step in the SET payment approval process that does not involve transmitting data through the public Internet.

Second Generation eCommerce. New technologies are providing companies with the ability to offer new levels of service to the marketplace.

Companies are using powerful new Web-based technologies to develop a second-generation of eCommerce tools to better manage relationships with their trading partners. Second-generation eCommerce web sites:

➢Provide a personalized interface.

➢Provide multiple forms of navigation. Both parametric navigation, which allows you to specify exactly what you are looking for, and conceptual navigation, which allows you to successively find closer approximations to what you are looking for.

➢Use forms of intelligence such as software agents.

➢Open up backroom systems to trading partners.

➢Chain together business transactions.

Thus by allowing business to do things that are impossible in the physical world they make the Internet a mission critical delivery channel.

Voice Over the Internet. A good example of second-generation eCommerce technology is offered by eFusion Corporation. eFusion products allow customers to conduct a telephone conversation with an organization's customer service representative over the same Internet connection as they are viewing the Web site.

For example, a customer who is looking at a supplier's Web site may have a question about which of two similar products is better suited to a particular application. Using this technology, the customer can contact a company representative who can answer questions (while they are still online), assist in placing the order, and offer additional related products. This gives suppliers the best of both worlds. It allows the speed and productivity of self-service through the Web site while still providing the flexibility and in-depth knowledge of customer service personnel in those special cases where it is required.

Open Buying on the Internet. Another good example of a second-generation eCommerce application is Open Buying on the Internet, or OBI. OBI addresses a need of business-to-business eCommerce that fundamentally differs from business-to-consumer eCommerce.

The following diagrams illustrate the problem as well as OBI's solution.

For typical consumer purchases on the Web, all that is needed is for the buyer to initiate the purchase. As long as the buyer's credit card is good, no further authorization is required. The Web server can approve the purchase.

For corporate purchases, the situation is not so simple. Purchases made for delivery to a formal receiving area may

Buying on the Internet—Consumer

not be received, and purchases to be paid by invoice may not be paid. The reason is simple. There is no record of a purchase order for the item purchased. Without a PO, receiving or accounts payable may reject the transaction.

This means that to ensure that items purchased on the Web are received and paid for, the information about that item must be rekeyed into the purchasing system.

This is hardly an elegant solution to the problem. The need to "double key" the data impacts productivity and allows opportunity for errors to creep into the process.

This is where OBI comes in. In an OBI scenario, both the buying and selling companies have OBI servers that can communicate with each other over the Web as well as with their own internal systems.

When a business using OBI with its supplier initiates a purchase through the Web, the selling company's Web server sends a purchase request through its OBI server and the buying company's OBI server to the buying company's purchasing system.

The buying company's purchasing system then determines whether this is an authorized purchase. Assuming that it is, the system will then automatically assign a PO number and transmit that PO number to the selling company as part of the purchase approval.

The selling company can then notify the buyer that the purchase has been approved, ship the product, and, if appropriate, invoice the customer. Both buyer and seller have the assurance that the shipment will be received and paid for as a properly authorized purchasing transaction. All this happens in a matter of seconds. At the same time, the buyer does not need to re-key any data to manage the transaction.

Buying on the Internet—Business

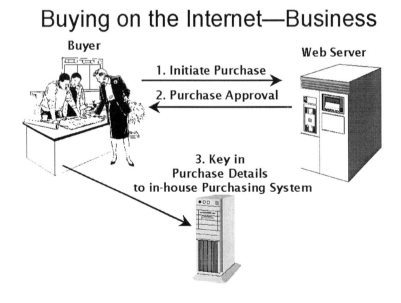

Buyer

Web Server

1. Initiate Purchase

2. Purchase Approval

3. Key in
Purchase Details
to in-house Purchasing System

Open Buying on the Internet

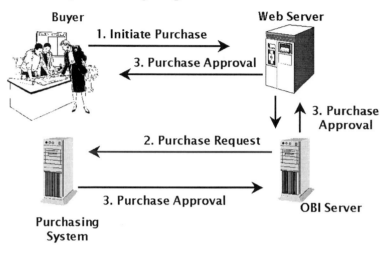

Buyer   Web Server

1. Initiate Purchase

3. Purchase Approval

3. Purchase Approval

2. Purchase Request

3. Purchase Approval

Purchasing System   OBI Server

Rules-based Software Agents and eXtensible Markup Language. It is likely that by the end of the year 2000 the total number of web sites in the world will be in the tens of millions. Given that situation, it's easy to see how a buyer could spend a tremendous amount of time just browsing the web. Therefore, it's not surprising that the latest technologies emerging from the software laboratories include rules-based software agents capable of navigating the World Wide Web on their own and negotiating with agent enabled web servers.

One of the most promising of such technologies is the use of eXtensible Markup Language (XML). Like HTML or Hypertext Markup Language — the current language of World Wide Web sites — it is a subset of SGML, the Standard Generalized Markup Language. Unlike HTML, it provides tags that allow sites to be "read" by business management systems in addition to humans. Systems that can interact with such sites promise to be some of the early examples of rules-based software agents.

Using one of these agents, a buyer can search the web for products and services meeting their specifications. Within a few minutes, the agent can scan thousands of web sites and report back to the buyer with those specific locations offering products and services best meeting the selection criteria. The buyer can click directly to those sites, review the available information, download videos, or execute virtual reality simulations, and make a buying decision. This sounds like we've described the ultimate in the sales and purchasing processes...but not quite.

Why not? Because there is no requirement that the "buyer" in the example above must be a human being. It could be a rules-based purchasing system that has detected a set of conditions established by management which require it to find a new source of supply. It may have received a requisition for an item that it has never before purchased, or the current suppliers of a given item may no longer be meeting management-defined requirements for quality or reliability. In either case, the rules-based purchasing system can make the determination to launch the agent and, in some cases, act on the information received from the agent without further human intervention being required.

The bottom line is that within a few years it will not be uncommon for companies using these technologies to go to the market with a request for quotation that says: "We are looking for suppliers who can provide products or services meeting these specifications and who can reply to this request within the next 90 seconds." That won't leave much time for the people in the marketing department to debate what price they should quote on each proposal.

Putting It All Together 7

Many companies have made especially effective strategic use of the World Wide Web and related eCommerce technologies. Let's take a quick look at some of the best:

Marshall Industries. Marshall Industries is a southern California-based distributor of electrical and electronics parts. Through a Web-based extranet, it allows 65,000 customers to select, order, and track 250,000 parts from 10,000 manufacturers. Marshall has created an on-line community in the electrical engineering field through their net seminars, online engineering news, and chat groups. If you're an electrical engineer and you don't log on to the Marshall Industries Web site at least a few times each month, you simply aren't keeping up with your professional reading. And, of course, if you are going to purchase parts, from which distributor do you think you might be just a little more likely to buy?

Marshall gives the lion's share of the credit to its extranet for the fact that business more than doubled during a four year period. And this was despite a reduction of about 10% in staff due to natural attrition.

AMP. AMP has a Web site from which they sell over 87,000 products. They distinguish themselves in a couple of important ways. First, they provide 3-D drawings of their products on their Web site. Second, they offer a picture search capability. This allows customers who know neither the correct name nor the product identification number to look up products by viewing a series of pictures which increasingly resemble the products they have. Finally, AMP is one of the few companies that fully appreciates that they are in a global market and reflects that in the design of their Web site. Their Web site is designed to support seven languages including the special characters necessary to support Chinese, Japanese, and Korean.

Amazon.com. Amazon.com is probably the best-known eCommerce site on the entire Web — and with good reason. Beyond the huge numbers of books, CDs, and other products available, beyond the explosive growth in sales and huge market valuation, lies some very powerful and effective technology that may apply to your organization as well.

Amazon starts by maintaining a personalized profile of every customer. This enables a number of powerful features.

First, Amazon provides for single click orders. This means that once a customer has established a profile, Amazon will know what default address the customer wishes their purchases shipped to, and what default credit card the customers wishes to use to pay. Thus, once a customer has selected an item, a single click is sufficient to order it.

Single click ordering makes it easy and time-efficient for the customer to buy. It also increases sales for Amazon. This is because fewer sales are lost to customers changing their minds while tediously entering their shipping and payment data.

Second, Amazon uses a technique called collaborative filtering to offer its customers recommendations. Even a first time customer who views an item will be told about other items that other customers who purchased the first item have also bought. This data is maintained in a massive database that allows instant cross-referencing from one item to others.

Once a customer has made several purchases, Amazon will present recommendations on arrival. By automatically reviewing a customer's recent purchases, Amazon's system makes recommendations based on which other items were purchased by others who also bought some or all of the returning customer's items. The customer then can review Amazon's recommendations and, if they choose, fine tune them by indicating items which the customer already has or did not like.

There is a wealth of opportunities to use this kind of technology in business sites. Most companies try to train customer service staff to cross sell. That is, to be certain to ask customers who order products A, B, or C if they don't also want to buy products X, Y, or Z. (For example, if a customer buys a toothbrush, the sales clerk should always ask if the customer needs toothpaste also.)

Because of employee inexperience and turnover, it can be very difficult to train for effective cross selling. Collaborative filtering technology can provide a service to customers while increasing productivity for customer service staff.

Amazon.com continues to push the envelope of easy to use, effective, and powerful eCommerce technology. Amazon is a business-to-consumer web site, but even if your environment is strictly business-to-business, there is much to learn from Amazon about sales and customer service on the Web.

Boeing. One very effective customer extranet is the Boeing Part Analysis & Requirement Tracking (PART) Page. It allows customers to check on inventory, get price quotes, check order status, and even specify the delivery warehouse for airplane parts purchased from Boeing. Boeing generated over $180 million in parts sales during the first full-year that the Boeing PART page was up and running. In addition, the site effectively increased their customer service from five days a week, eight hours a day to seven days a week, 24 hours a day without any increase in staff. At the same time, they reduced delivery cycle time, order errors, and delivery unit costs.

One useful function of the Boeing PART Page is its "Replaced By" feature. This feature allows customers to immediately see whether currently installed parts have been replaced by new ones.

This function may have led to an interesting development related by Tom Dimarco, Director, Spares Systems, for Boeing. Tom says that the PART Page was originally designed to allow the many smaller airlines and repair facilities who were not already using EDI with Boeing to have online access.

Much to the surprise of those at Boeing, many orders coming into the PART Page were from the large airlines who already had EDI links. Tom and his associates wondered why buyers whose systems were already linked electronically to Boeing would bother to log onto the Web and enter orders through the PART Page.

It seems that, as airline parts buyers discovered the PART Page (perhaps through functions like the Replaced By feature), they began ordering directly from Boeing online. Buyers recognized that Boeing could provide a ready-to-assemble "kit" of parts for a high-priority maintenance activity much more quickly and cost-effectively than the individual items could be obtained from different sources, including sources within the airline's own system.

In many cases, a particular maintenance job might require many different kinds of parts. Those parts, though they might be in the airline's in-house inventory, could be scattered all over the country. It could take many hours or even days to round up all the necessary parts.

Two key tools of automation contribute to this time and cost saving capability. The first is the rules-based real-time

Boeing SONIC (Spares Ordering and Nonstop Inventory Control) system that processes orders entirely without human intervention unless boundary limits (for example, credit limit) are broken. The second is the Boeing PART Page that permits the customer to see the SONIC databases directly so they can determine part availability and order status. Airline parts buyers can assemble their "kit", based on the mechanic's needs, in real time directly on Boeing's Web site. The SONIC system generates the pick and ship paperwork in the appropriate Boeing distribution center and the parts are shipped within two hours.

With Boeing's commitment to shipping parts within two hours, mechanics found they could anticipate receiving all the parts they needed for an entire job in one shipment — often much more quickly than they could expect from within their own organization. When an airplane is grounded, at a cost of thousands of dollars an hour, every minute is precious.

The lesson here is a powerful one. Provide customers with functions and features they may have a use for, and they, in turn, will get creative in how they use those capabilities. By effectively doing so, Boeing was able to discover, and satisfy, a previously unrecognized need in the marketplace.

Cisco. Cisco is the world's leading manufacturer of data communications routers. It has over 50,000 registered users on its extranet. In 1997, the first full year the extranet was on line, Cisco became the first company in history to generate more than one billion dollars in sales via the World Wide Web. This represented over 20 percent of Cisco's sales for that year.

Cisco has also saved over $270 million in customer support expenses using its extranet. One hundred million dollars of those savings have been the reduced cost of paper documentation alone. But perhaps the most powerful aspect of Cisco's extranet has been its on-line configuration agent.

A data communications router must be customized to the specific hardware, operating system, and network environment in which it will be used. Cisco's online configuration agent allows systems engineers to specify their requirements. The agent then provides the most cost-effective configuration that will meet those requirements. This, of course, provides Cisco with a strong competitive advantage. But the advantage goes beyond that.

The configuration agent is fully integrated with Cisco's internal business management systems. Thus, when an engineer makes the decision to purchase the recommended configuration, their click on the "Submit Order" button sets off a chain reaction of information handling within Cisco's systems.

The configuration agent passes the order into the Customer Order Management system, which immediately updates the Master Production Scheduling system. That, in turn, drives production requirements into the Materials Requirements Planning system which passes requisitions into the Procurement system which then generates electronic POs and releases to suppliers.

Similarly, the Order Management system updates the Finished Goods Inventory and Distribution Requirements Planning systems. A single click of a button by a customer sends electronic ripples moving throughout the Cisco organization and, indeed, throughout the industry. This integration of the World Wide Web with internal business management systems and processes represents one of the leading examples of true digital transformation of a business.

National Semiconductor. National Semiconductor is well known as a manufacturer of integrated circuits and related products. It has taken customer service to new highs via its sophisticated extranet. National has designed areas of its Web site to meet the specific needs of customers' purchasing agents, design engineers, and quality control managers. But National is moving beyond that to provide mass personalization on its Web site.

According to Phil Gibson, Director of Interactive Marketing, customer contacts went from 200 per month in the 1950s and 1960s when personal sales calls were required, to 25,000 in the 1980s through telephone call centers. In the 1990s, National has been able to increase customer contacts to 750,000 per month through its Web site. Now National is taking the next step beyond customer self-service — mass personalization.

One way in which it is doing this is through buyer bulletins. A buyer bulletin allows a customer to specify particular parts or products needed for one or more current projects. Customers may also specify the distributors through which they prefer to have their National products delivered.

Every night, each distributor transmits inventory levels for each National product to National's website using file transfers and scripts. The next day, when the customer accesses their buyer bulletin, they are provided a list of specified distributors who have the identified products in stock.

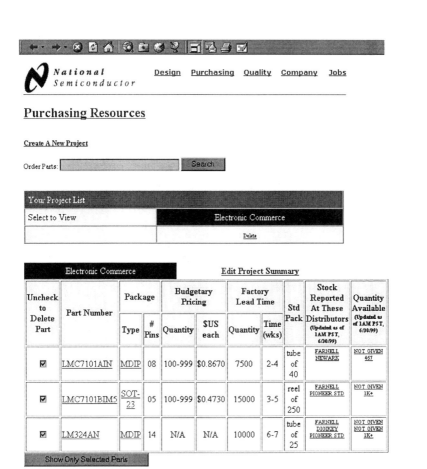

Design   Purchasing   Quality   Company   Jobs

Purchasing Resources

Create A New Project

Order Parts: [   ] Search

Your Project List

Select to View	Electronic Commerce
	Delete

| Electronic Commerce | | | | | | | | | Edit Project Summary |

Uncheck to Delete Part	Part Number	Package		Budgetary Pricing		Factory Lead Time		Std Pack	Stock Reported At These Distributors (Updated as of 1AM PST, 6/30/99)	Quantity Available (Updated as of 1AM PST, 6/30/99)
		Type	# Pins	Quantity	$US each	Quantity	Time (wks)			
☑	LMC7101AIN	MDIP	08	100-999	$0.8670	7500	2-4	tube of 40	FARNELL NEWARK	NOT GIVEN 467
☑	LMC7101BIM5	SOT-23	05	100-999	$0.4730	15000	3-5	reel of 250	FARNELL PIONEER STD	NOT GIVEN 1K+
☑	LM324AN	MDIP	14	N/A	N/A	10000	6-7	tube of 25	FARNELL DIGIKEY PIONEER STD	NOT GIVEN NOT GIVEN 1K+

Show Only Selected Parts

This distributor list includes a live link to the distributor's Web site. The customer clicks on that link and is taken directly to the distributor's order form with the order already filled out for the desired product. All the customer needs to do is enter the quantity and the order can be processed immediately.

For those few, large, national accounts that purchase directly from National, customization is taken one step farther. Each major customer is provided a customized Web site. The customization is done by national accounts sales representatives working closely with their marketing team. They use a simple Web design tool developed by National's technology group. This allows National's sales force to make information available to key customers that they may not wish to publish on their Web site for the world to see. For example, they can provide the status of new products which are under development, or contact information for key individuals within the National Semiconductor organization.

Gibson says, "We want to work through our distributors. They provide valuable services to many of our customers that we are unable to provide directly ourselves. We do not see the World Wide Web as a tool that will disintermediate distributors. At the same time, it is certainly clear that those distributors who rapidly adopt key electronic commerce technologies will have a tremendous competitive advantage over those who do not."

Caterpillar. In many industries, companies are working cooperatively to develop industry-wide extranets. One of the best examples is taking place in the heavy equipment industry through Caterpillar Tractor's Enhanced Product Realization project. This project integrates the use of real-time multimedia tools such as audio and video teleconferencing and electronic white boards over the Internet with design tools such as CAD/CAM, computer-aided engineering applications, and product data management systems. The business objective is to reduce the time required to design, develop, and deliver new parts from the traditional five to six months to just five days. Here is a typical five-day scenario:

> ***Day one:*** New soil conditions require modifications to a tractor undercarriage. The customer telephones and sends a fax to the dealer who forwards the information to the regional office. There it is scanned into the system and passed through the Internet to the Caterpillar agricultural products support group. The team leader logs the request and schedules a late day

electronic conference. The team leader creates an online file folder with spreadsheets, charts, documents, databases, and drawings from engineering, manufacturing, suppliers, and product support. The team sets up a work plan with milestones, tasks, time, and resources. The team leader emails the plan to the dealer.

Day two: During a morning electronic conference the team makes decisions about its approach. The team leader makes the duty assignments and updates the work plan. At the end of the day, the team meets again and decides to design a new component. Design alternatives are discussed and assessed.

Day three: In the morning the testing supplier provides details about their ability to make the requested modifications. Through email and videoconferences the team refines the design alternatives, taking into consideration the supplier's input. At the end of the day the team compares the design analysis results. It then selects an option for casting.

Day four: The team finalizes the changes and the workflow. The team leader checks with the supplier on the pouring of the casting.

Day five: The supplier delivers the casting to Caterpillar for final machining. Caterpillar ships the part to the dealer for installation on the customer's tractor. All information is captured for future reference.

Associated Equipment Distributors. Another powerful example of industry cooperation is the Construction Equipment Support Network developed for the construction equipment industry by the Associated Equipment Distributors and the Construction Industry Manufacturers Association. This system is designed to support the needs of equipment dealers in providing product support for their manufacturers' products.

As shown in the diagram below, the system has three major components:
➤ The dealer's 3rd party business management system,
➤ An electronic parts catalog, and
➤ A dealer communications facility.

The parts catalog can be accessed from the Internet or distributed on CD-ROM. Information on the Web is real time and maintained by the manufacturer. The system is

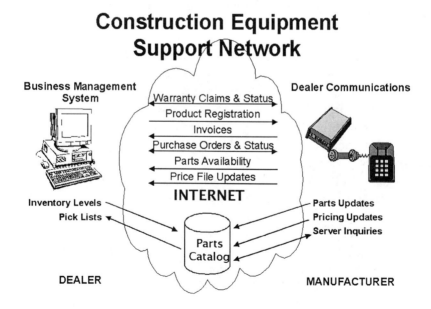

Construction Equipment Support Network

Business Management System

Dealer Communications

Warranty Claims & Status
Product Registration
Invoices
Purchase Orders & Status
Parts Availability
Price File Updates
INTERNET

Inventory Levels
Pick Lists

Parts Catalog

Parts Updates
Pricing Updates
Server Inquiries

DEALER

MANUFACTURER

designed to meet the needs of multi-line dealers allowing multiple manufacturers' data to be viewed from a common user interface. The dealer can look up the necessary parts by name or part number and machine serial number. They can also look up parts by viewing a drawing delineating the equipment's parts in detail. By clicking a given part on the drawing, the dealer can pull up its name, part number and specifications.

When the dealer removes a part from the warehouse shelf for a repair or to ship to a customer, the parts catalog will pass the pick list information to the dealer's business management system to update inventory levels.

Using EDI, the dealer's business management system sends purchase order information to the manufacturer to replenish supply. Parts pricing and availability are updated on the Web site and passed to the distributor's business management system. Order status is available online through a standard Web browser, as is electronic transmission of standard EDI transactions. The dealer can also electronically receive invoices, register products, file warranty claims, and follow up on their status.

The Air Transport Association (ATA). ATA is working with Continental DataGraphics to implement a similar initiative. Under this initiative, those maintaining or repairing aircraft will have online access to a single catalog of parts from virtually all aerospace manufacturers. Maintenance personnel can identify, access, and display all information required to repair or maintain a part through a single seamless interface. The users first access an Illustrated Parts Catalog, or IPC.

Distributed electronically as a database of parts records and intelligent graphics, the Smart IPC™ can be viewed via Web browsers. It allows users to hyperlink between parts list items and intelligent graphics. The system is designed to

allow non-programmers to publish updates to the IPC in real time. This way mechanics and others accessing the system will see the latest parts as soon as they are available.

Once the mechanic has identified the part they need, a single click will take them to Continental DataGraphics' Smart Shop online ordering facility.

Using Smart Shop, mechanics can then place orders, check on order status, and perform other useful functions. Smart Shop also provides links to the ATA's SPEC 2000 industry marketplace databases of new OEM parts listings, surplus parts listings, and listings of repair facilities categorized according to each facility's specific parts repair capabilities. These databases provide a "one stop" view of all available parts and repair services from multiple manufacturers and

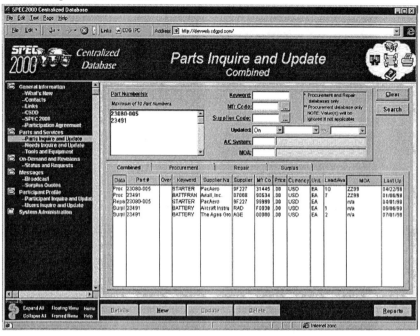

suppliers. The SPEC 2000 industry marketplace will also eventually allow for online funds transfer and will use an authentication server, hardware and software tokens, digital certificates and digital signatures to provide robust security measures.

Service Industries and Government 8

Many people are under the impression that eCommerce is just for tangible products. That is, only manufacturers, distributors, and retailers of physical items can benefit from using eCommerce. Nothing could be farther from the truth.

Service organizations in many industries effectively use eCommerce and the Internet to generate additional revenues and provide a higher level of service for their customers or constituents. These industries include banking, credit unions, insurance, and government at all levels. Lets take a look at some of the better examples of how organizations in these industries are using eCommerce.

Online Banking. Online banking is exploding among not only banks, but savings and loans, credit unions and other financial institutions.

There are several reasons people like to bank online:

➤ They can readily see their current bank balances whether they have their checkbooks with them or not.

➤ Account reconciliation is much faster and easier than with traditional paper-based reconciliation.

➤ Online bill payment allows individuals and small business owners to ensure that their bills are paid on a timely basis even when they're out of the office.

➤ The use of debit cards, combined with online banking allows people to track their expenses automatically without having to keep cash receipts and make separate bookkeeping entries.

➢ Online bill presentment eliminates the need for consumers to track or enter bills to be paid into their records.

With online bill presentment, large organizations that deal directly with consumers send billing information via EDI to a third party financial services company such as CheckFree. The third party transmits the data to the appropriate financial institution for each consumer billed. Users download their bills from their banks along with their checking account information and have it entered directly into their accounting system.

Because the benefits to consumers and small businesses are so significant, it's not surprising that many banks, credit unions, and other financial institutions are offering these services. But the financial sector is not new to eCommerce. Since the mid-1980s money center banks have offered financial EDI services to their corporate customers. Some of the more commonly used transactions are shown in the chart below.

Financial EDI Messages

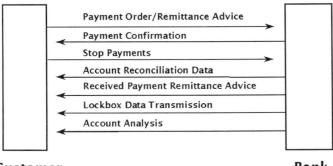

Payment Order/Remittance Advice

Payment Confirmation

Stop Payments

Account Reconciliation Data

Received Payment Remittance Advice

Lockbox Data Transmission

Account Analysis

Customer   **Bank**

Financial EDI will continue to be an important service for financial institutions to offer to their large customers. Now with new Internet-based services, banks can extend similar offerings to their small business customers and to their individual customers.

Many financial institutions have extended their services to their markets by acting as Internet portals. They offer such tools as:

> Links to news and weather
> Professional news services
> Personnel announcements
> Relevant legal rulings
> Information on new products and services
> Financial advice

One of the best examples of this is Farm Credit Services, a subsidiary of the Farm Credit Association of the Seventh District, based in Minneapolis. It offers a customizable portal for members that provides news, agricultural information, agricultural market data, weather, and agricultural technology information. This is all in addition to secure access to customers' farm financing account information.

Insurance on the Web. Insurance and insurance-related services are rapidly moving to the Web. According to a survey by Conning and Company, online sales of home, auto, and life insurance surpassed the $1 billion mark in premiums by 2000 and is expected to exceed $6 billion by 2006.

Another survey by IVANS in 1998 showed that at least 50% of consumers were willing to file insurance claims online. Now, with the increased use of the Internet, and growing consumer comfort with and confidence in online transactions, that percentage has grown significantly.

Leading insurance organizations have not missed the message. Companies such as MetLife and New York Life offer personalized advice online. Liberty Mutual provides insurance-related "coaching" through such major life events as marriage, the birth of children, retirement, etc. By becoming "infomediaries", these organizations hope to build a loyal customer base — one that will return often to their Web site even when they aren't looking to purchase insurance.

Direct sales of insurance on the Web are increasing dramatically. Unlike tangible products such as books or computers, insurance can actually be "delivered" online. John Hancock's MarketPlace allows consumers to buy certain coverages directly online. Progressive Insurance offers online sales of its auto and related insurance. Affinity Insurance Services even allows members of client organizations such as the Nurses Service Organization to purchase professional liability insurance online and pay their premiums with a credit card.

Virtual communities with common interests have become effective launching points for relevant online insurance sales. For example, former Surgeon General C. Everett Koop's health care portal has a Personal Insurance Center where visitors can compare health care related coverages and even get rate quotes online. Quicken's InsureMarket allows users of the financial software to evaluate and purchase insurance. And insurance industry specialty sites such as InsWeb offer online quotes for a variety of insurance coverages.

Government eCommerce. eCommerce in government is proliferating at both the state and federal levels. Various federal agencies such as the Department of Defense, the Department of Veterans Affairs, the General Services Administration, the Health Care Financing Administration, and the IRS have been using EDI for many years. However, the advent of the Web has allowed governmental organizations to reach out much more effectively to their constituents. Recently, state governments have started making widespread use of eCommerce.

The State of Pennsylvania provides residents with downloadable forms for income, property, and corporate taxes. It offers online voter registration and auto licensing, titling, and registration. Individuals may purchase fishing licenses online. Residents may access extensive school profiles, county-by-county listings of where to register and launch boats, and online job listings.

Connecticut's ConneCT site gets over 300,000 hits per day. It provides access to legislative, judicial, and executive agencies; to schools, technical colleges, and universities; and to more than 100 municipalities. Interested parties can access the University of Connecticut's statewide Geo-Spatial Data Library or listings of available commercial and industrial properties (maintained by the Connecticut Economic Resource Center). The site also provides a legislative-bill search engine as well as a downloadable archive covering 13 years of decisions by the state Freedom of Information Commission.

Arkansas has a clever Web-based tool called Lobbyist in a Box. It allows interested persons to monitor legislative activity. Users can track specific legislation subject areas, or legislation sponsored by key committees or legislators. It's updated daily and users can be notified via the Lobbyist in a Box home page or by email of relevant legislative activity.

This is just one of several state government sites developed by the Atlanta-based National Information Consortium. Others include Georgia, Indiana, Iowa, Kansas, and Virginia.

GeorgiaNet, the State of Georgia site, utilizes the first electronic commerce digital signature application in Georgia. It allows for online filing of Georgia Residential Mortgage Act Fee Statements by mortgage lenders and brokers with the Georgia Department of Banking and Finance. Users file statements electronically using a digital signature, send their digitally signed documents to the state over the Internet, and electronically transfer the fee securely from their bank account to the state. These brokers and lenders access a secure site to apply for and receive digital signature keys.

The Georgia State Board of Professional Engineers also allows engineers to access an online renewal form through GeorgiaNet. Engineers can make any necessary corrections to their application, pay fees through a secured credit card transaction, receive electronic confirmation of their renewal, and print their renewal form for their records.

Through Indiana's Access Indiana Network, the Department of Motor Vehicles provides online automobile registration. Automobile owners use the state's Rapid Renewal System to electronically submit a vehicle registration renewal notice. Vehicle owners are assigned a PIN to enter the system which uses secure encryption to prevent credit card fraud. The system verifies payment and then submits the renewal request to the Bureau of Motor Vehicles (BMV) for processing.

The Commonwealth of Virginia offers a Governmental Meetings Calendar. It serves as a bulletin board for announcing public government meetings. Virginia also allows any organization planning a public meeting to list its meeting on the calendar.

Designing Your eBusiness Strategy 9

eCommerce is much more than an enabling technology that organizations can choose to use to change how they do business. It is a driving force for digital transformation. It means only those companies that master the use of these tools and technologies in order to transform themselves into eBusinesses can hope to survive the transition from the industrial economy of the 20th Century to the digital economy of the 21st Century. So, what steps do you take?

Start by accepting that change is not what it used to be. Change has become a process; it has become a permanent part of the external environment. The only way that companies can manage change rather than having change manage them is by dedicating people and resources to managing change as a permanent part of their internal organization.

Senior management's role is critical and not one that can be delegated down through the company ranks. It's up to senior management to manage the human side of change for two reasons. First, it is strategically critical, and therefore not cheap. It requires significant investment, but the return will be outstanding. Second, redesigning business processes implies crossing old departmental boundaries.

It is not feasible for companies to take an idea such as Continuous Replenishment and permit the accounting staff to say, "We think this is a great idea," and have the shipping personnel say, "We're not so sure. You implement your piece of it and see how it works. Then we'll decide whether we're going to do it." eBusiness brings with it changes that cross departmental boundaries and therefore require all parties to participate or the benefits are lost.

It's up to senior management to change organizational beliefs and understandings. Top management must assure people, "Yes, it is okay to change the way that we do business." It is up to top management to change organizational culture, behaviors, and even structure.

Doesn't it make sense to develop an overall corporate strategy for digitally transforming your organization into an eBusiness? Rather than focusing on specific technologies such as bar coding or the World Wide Web, or on particular applications such as customer service or procurement, you should look at your business as a whole.

Begin by staffing and organizing for the future. In the digital economy of the 21st Century, successful companies will have 10 percent of their staffs managing change. Change-management encompasses such functions as business modelling and business process design, electronic commerce, and information technology management. The objective is to invest 10 percent of your people's time and effort into ensuring that your business models, processes, and systems are most effectively structured for use by the other 90 percent of your people. In the future, change-management will be every bit as mission critical a business process as order fulfillment or human resource management is today.

Similarly, successful organizations in the digital economy will have their employees spending 10 percent of their time being educated and trained as to how do their jobs more effectively the other 90 percent of the time.

If, as a reader of this book, you are concerned as to whether the management of your organization is investing as required in education and change-management, don't worry too much, because if they don't, the new owners soon will.

A cartoon appeared recently showing a mother asking the father to check on their teenage son. He went upstairs, looked over his son's shoulder at his computer, and asked his son what he was doing. The son replied that he was, "adding some hot links and Java scripting to my home page." When his wife queried him on his return, the father said, "I don't know. All he said was something about sausages and coffee."

Unfortunately, this cartoon accurately reflects how well even sophisticated business persons understand current business technology.

This was brought home very clearly in a survey done by a major news magazine which asked the participants to explain what a modem does. Two control groups were questioned—sixth graders and Fortune 1000 executives. Of the sixth graders, 93% could accurately explain what a modem does. Only 23% of the executives could do the same!

Can Explain What a Modem Does

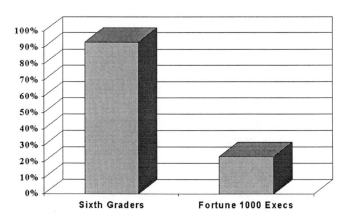

Executives need to understand not only the terminology, but, more importantly, the business implication of eCommerce technologies.

Executive education is an important first step in change-management, but only part of developing your overall eBusiness strategy.

Develop Your Strategy. The steps needed to develop your eBusiness strategy are:

1. Senior Management Education — Senior management must understand and be committed to investing the resources needed to gain the benefits of eCommerce and eBusiness. This is not a technical issue and cannot be delegated to the data processing department. It demands the understanding, commitment, and active participation of top management.

2. Organization — The right person or people from the organization must be selected to manage the strategic planning and implementation process for eBusiness. Include key individuals who represent a cross-section of business processes plus information technology management. The exact number of people depends on the size and complexity of the organization, but typically there will be 5–10 team members.

The important thing is to get the right people on the team. Remember that the people who have time to work on digital transformation are not the ones who need to be doing it. The right people are usually extremely busy. It's senior management's responsibility to free them up to focus on the future of the business.

3. Staff and Educate an eBusiness Project Team — In a very small business, the project team may be a single person. In a large corporation, it may be an interdisciplinary group of as many as a dozen people. No matter the size, the team members must all understand the information technologies available and their impact on business processes before they can electronically transform those processes.

If your Project Team is large enough, split it into task groups, which should be carefully coordinated, to address the issues below. If your project team is small, it will need to address these areas concurrently.

4. *Address Simultaneous Efforts* — After developing and educating an eBusiness project team, team members will need to address three simultaneous efforts.

➤**Do the basic blocking and tackling**

➤**Work with the technology**

➤**Develop the vision**

Do the basic blocking and tackling. Get your existing processes and systems working effectively. For example, have bar coding in place with a well-structured, standard product numbering scheme. Your inventory <u>must</u> be under control.

Work with the technology. Provide each employee with a networked station (or for warehouse or factory floor personnel, easy access to one). Your corporate network should tie together all workstations and business management systems. At the same time, begin experimenting with low-profile applications of such technologies as internal and external email, Web sites, intranets, electronic forms, and EDI.

Get your basic blocking and tackling taken care of and begin working with new technologies at the same time that you are developing your vision. For most companies, this should require a period of about six to eighteen months. Once the vision is clear, the basic blocking and tackling is underway, and you have begun to develop some comfort with the new technologies, then you will be ready to implement your vision.

Develop the vision. Look out three to five years and ask yourself:

➤What will our industry look like as it changes to meet the demands of the digital economy? (our digital industry model)

➤How can we best leverage our core competencies in the digital industry environment we anticipate in a few years time? (our business model)

➤How will our business processes support our business model?

➤What people skills will we need to manage new business processes?

➤How should we be organized to use people skills to best effect?

➤What will our infostructure, or information technology infrastructure, need to look like to support our new digital business processes?

Developing this kind of vision requires an open mind and a broad perspective. There's no substitute for personal education. At the end of this book you'll find a list of required reading for executives planning for survival and success in the Digital Jungle.

The part of your project team that is developing your eBusiness vision will need to do the following:

Describe your Digital Industry Model — This is a description of how your industry might be functioning in the digital economy of the 21st Century.

Design your Digital Business Model — This defines the ways in which your company will leverage its core competencies within the digital industry environment found in your digital industry model. It shows where you'll use content, context, or infostructure to add value for customers.

Plan Process Redesign — A high-level redesign of top priority business processes must be mapped out. The objective is to automate the routine transactions and common exceptions (within limits defined by management). Then you can use tools such as workflow automation to automate the exception handling that requires human intervention. Finally, build into your new process designs the ability to capture performance statistics. This way you can measure performance on an ongoing basis and apply total quality and continuous improvement principles to those newly redesigned business processes.

Review and Revise Your Organizational Structure — Once you've redesigned your business processes to support your digital business model, you can then identify what people skills will be needed to managed those processes. This in turn will help determine what organizational structure is most effective for those skill sets.

Assess and Design Your Information Technology Infrastructure — Your infrastructure is the architecture of the hardware, software, and networks needed to support your digitally redesigned business processes. Only after you understand those processes and their requirements can you effectively design that infrastructure.

Once you've developed your eBusiness vision, you will need to:

5. Educate Employees —This is a key to successful eBusiness. Employees must understand in advance what changes are going to take place, how those changes affect them, and their role in the change process. Effective employee education is not a one-shot deal. Remember that in successful organizations each employee spends 10 percent of his or her time on an ongoing basis learning how to better do his or her job the other 90 percent of the time.

6. Market to Achieve Critical Mass — You must market the benefits of doing business electronically to your trading partners. The objective is to get to a critical mass of business transactions as rapidly as possible. Critical mass is that point where most information entering a business process comes in electronically, and human intervention is required only for exceptions.

7. Conduct Ongoing Strategic Review — Changes in a company's internal and external environment impact long-term priorities. A sound eBusiness strategy looks two to five years down the road. No organization can afford to cast its strategy in concrete for that long. It's critical to have a clearly defined long-term direction; however, it cannot be inflexible. This is why leading organizations review their strategy annually, fine-tuning and, if necessary, redirecting it.

Success in the Digital Economy

10

Be proactive — not reactive. If you wait until you're forced to embrace digital transformation, it's too late. You don't have to jump into the deep end with your eyes closed and your hands tied behind your back. If you begin the planning process now, you have time to do it right. Begin taking steps now that will lay the groundwork for the changes to your business models and business processes so that you can compete more effectively.

Once you've developed your eBusiness strategy, you can develop your long-term implementation plan and the short-term action plan to kick it off. It's important to review the company as a whole.

While costs and benefits are usually associated with specific process areas of your company, many of the key costs in enhancing your company's core technological capabilities cross all processes. Think of your technological capabilities as a corporate asset. If you only look at one functional area at a time, you get into the old game of which area of the company gets saddled with the investment for the whole company. In this kind of situation, what happens in most companies is that the project never happens at all.

To develop your eBusiness priorities, you must step back and look at the entire business. The Digital Transformation Timeline below graphically represents a corporate eBusiness strategy. The horizontal bars on the bottom represent your eBusiness policies and procedures, and, above that, your core technological capability. The vertical bars on the top represent the mission critical business processes of your organization.

In this diagram, time moves from left to right. A fundamental part of your eBusiness strategy is to determine what eBusiness policies and procedures you'll need to put in place. These should be flexible enough to accommodate change. At the same time, these are long-term policies and procedures, so it's not desirable to plan at the outset to change them. Questions to answer in developing your eBusiness policies and procedures should include:

➤ Who is responsible for and authorized to approve changes to company business practices?

➤ How will these changes be funded and who will approve the funding?

➤ How will we ensure that new eBusiness practices are soundly designed from a legal, audit, and security perspective?

➤ How will we integrate our eBusiness strategy with our overall information technology, human resources, marketing, and financial strategies?

Your eBusiness strategy must also identify how you're going to evolve your core technological capabilities. This consists of the combination of your IT infrastructure and the skills of your people in utilizing the available technology tools. It is this combination that allows you to digitally transform your current business practices into eBusiness processes.

But don't get the cart ahead of the horse. It is the needs of your eBusiness processes that should drive the evolution of your core technological capability and not the other way around. At the same time you must be realistic about how quickly you can implement change in your core technological capability.

For example it's likely to take a minimum of a year, and perhaps considerably longer, for a company not experienced in the relevant technologies to implement an extranet secured with public key encryption and integrated with both legacy applications and work flow automation.

The vertical bars at the top of the timeline pictured below reflect the sequence in which you'll transform your current business processes into eBusiness processes. Ideally, the changes that will bring about the greatest return on investment should be done first. But many other factors come into play.

As described above, the process with the best theoretical ROI may require core technological capability that would take a year or two to put into place. In that case, it may be desirable to defer that project. Instead, you may wish to undertake a project you can implement with only minimal changes to your current core technological capability. Or, you may find that it makes no sense to try to undertake a high return project unless you first address a related process — even if the return on the first process is lower.

Digital Transformation Timeline

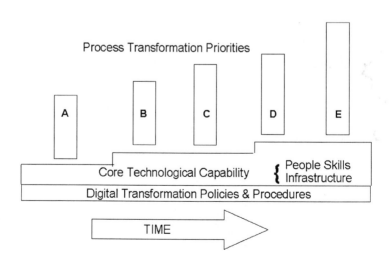

Process Transformation Priorities

Finally, other things being equal, you should implement the smallest, easiest project first. It's best to start with an easy win. It builds confidence in the approach and among the people in your organization. The approach described here ensures that while you may gather low hanging fruit first, you'll do it in a way that lays a proper foundation for future changes that may return even more to your business.

By the time you reach the end of the eBusiness transformation process you will have changed the business as a whole to be functional in a digital economy. This is not the end of the journey because the eBusiness transformation process must continue indefinitely. You will, however, have made the initial steps for survival and success.

When it comes to reacting to the demands of your customers and the threats of current and potential new

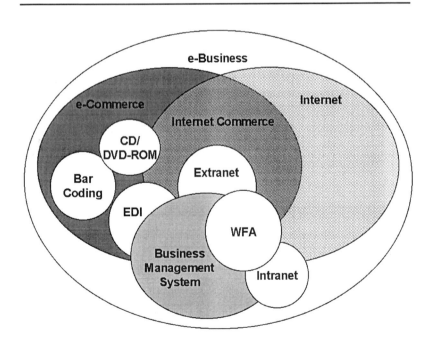

competitors by digitally transforming your business, the choice is not whether, but how to do it. You can be reactive and spend the absolute minimal amount necessary to satisfy short-term demands and competitive threats. But if you do that, in a few years you will find that you have spent as much if not more money, time, and effort in reacting to short-term outside forces while gaining little if any strategic advantage.

Or, you can recognize that you must spend the money, and invest the time and effort necessary, to make changes to your business. By being proactive, you can provide more value to your customers and build strategic relations with suppliers and other key trading partners. You can reduce your costs and cycle times, as well as improve quality, increase productivity, and gain the long-term competitive and strategic advantages that will ensure your organization not only survives but thrives in the 21st Century's Digital Jungle.

Suggested Reading List

The books on this list can be purchased over the Web. Please access the eCommerce Bookstore at www.e-com.com/ecommercebooks.htm for more information.

Being Digital, by Nicholas Negroponte

Business at the Speed of Thought, by Bill Gates

Competing for the Future, by Gary Hamel & C. K. Prahalad

Customer Service on the Internet, by Jim Sterne

Cybercorp, by James Martin

Doing Business in the Information Age, by Jack Shaw

Getting Started With Bar Codes, by Rick Bushnell

If It Ain't Broke, Break It, by Robert Kriegel

Net Income, by Wally Bock & Jeff Senne

Reengineering the Corporation, by Michael Hammer and James Champy

The Digital Economy, by Don Tapscott

The Road Ahead, by Bill Gates

World Wide Web Marketing, by Jim Sterne

Unbounding the Future, by Eric Drexler

Glossary

Business model: represents the combination of business processes that comprise your enterprise.

Business process: a group of related activities that provide value to the customer.

Content: the products or services offered.

Context: where the buyer meets the seller and an exchange of value takes place.

Core competencies: skills or aptitudes that provide value to your customers, differentiate your firm from the competition, and can extend to new products, services, and markets.

Digital industry model: an industry model based on digital relationships.

eBusiness: the use of digital technologies as enablers to transform business models and processes in ways not possible with traditional paper-bound communications.

eCommerce: the use of electronic information technologies to improve business relationships between trading partners.

Electronic Data Interchange (EDI): the exchange of information between automated business management systems without human intervention.

Electronic Forms Routing and Approval (EFRA): the exchange of structured business information (forms) among people and business management systems across a network.

Electronic Funds Transfer (EFT): the electronic transfer of funds and related payment information between banks or other financial institutions.

Email: any system which provides the ability for computer users to create, send and receive electronic messages and associated electronic documents.

Encryption: a security measure similar to the authentication method except that the actual message is scrambled. Encryption is typically used for highly sensitive data such as payment information.

Evaluated Receipts Settlements (ERS): a payment method in which payment is triggered by the receipt of goods rather than by receipt of an invoice.

eXtensible Markup Language (XML): like HTML (Hypertext Markup Language), XML is an outgrowth of SGML (Standard Generalized Markup Language) that permits developers to control and display data in the same way they control text and graphics. XML is not a replacement for HTML.

Extranet: a close relative of an intranet with the difference being that both specified trading partners and remote company offices not confined to the corporate location can securely access it via the internet.

Hypertext links (Hyperlinks): a means of "jumping" from one information site to another on the same or different network server; a link between one document and another, related documents elsewhere in a collection. By clicking on a word or phrase that has been highlighted on a computer screen, a user can jump directly to files related to that subject.

Intranet: a private internal network that operates within a company and is usually insulated from the outside world via an electronic or hardware impedance called a firewall.

Non-repudiation: provides a means whereby the sender of a document cannot disclaim having sent it, nor can the receiver of the document deny having received it.

Open Buying on the Internet (OBI): a business practice designed to enhance the ease of purchasing on the Web for businesses. On receiving a purchase request, a Web server transmits the information to the buyer's procurement system via OBI servers that both companies use. If the purchase is approved, a PO number and other data are transmitted back to the Web server. The Web server then notifies the buyer that the product will be delivered.

Process redesign: rethinking and redesign of businesses to achieve dramatic improvements.

Public Key Encryption: a means of uniquely identifying an individual to others. Can be stored on a smart card or computer ring and released through voiceprint or fingerprint identification.

Radio Frequency Identification (RFI): a form of data capture using radio waves to transmit non-optical automatic identification.

Standard General Markup Language (SGML): an international standard for defining special document types and controlling presentation of pages. HTML (Hypertext Markup Language) is an instance of SGML.

Trading partner: any person or organization outside of your own with whom you exchange information in order to conduct business (e.g. customers, suppliers, employees, banks, transportation carriers, etc.).

Web-to-EDI translators: allows smaller or less sophisticated trading partners to enter information on a Web form that is translated into an EDI transmission upon submission.

Workflow Automation (WFA): the electronic routing of documents and data among people and business management systems to speed information flows and enhance decision making and exception management within a business process.

XML: see extensible markup language.

World Wide Web References

You may want to check out Web sites of the companies referenced in this book. They are listed below. You will find the most updated version of this list on the Electronic Commerce Strategies Web site at www.e-com.com

Air Transport Association (ATA), **www.air-transport.org**

Amazon.com, **www.amazon.com**

AMP, **www.amp.com**

Associated Equipment Distributors (AED), **www.aednet.org**

Boeing PART Page, **www.boeing.com/assocproducts**

Caterpillar, **www.caterpillar.com**

CheckFree, **www.checkfree.com**

Cisco, **www.cisco.com**

Construction Industry Manufacturers Association (CIMA),
  www.cimanet.com

Continental DataGraphics, **www.cdgl.com**

Dell Computers, **www.dell.com**

Data Interchange Standards Association (DISA), **www.disa.org**

eFusion, **www.efusion.com**

Encyclopedia Britannica, **www.britannica.com**

Farm Credit Services, **www.farmcredit.com**

Federal Express, **www.fedex.com**

Georgia State Board of Professional Engineers,
  www.sos.state.ga.us/ebd-pels

GeorgiaNet, **www.ganet.state.ga.us**

InsWeb, **www.insweb.com**

John Hancock, **www.hancock.com**

Kmart, **www.kmart.com**

Levi's, **www.levistrauss.com**

Liberty Mutual, **www.libertymutual.com**

Marshall Industries, **www.marshall.com**

MetLife, **www.metlife.com**

National Information Consortium, **www.state-info.com**
National Semiconductor, **www.national.com**
New York Life, **www.newyorklife.com**
Nurses Service Organization, **www.nso.com**
OBI Consortium, **www.openbuy.org**
Pennzoil, **www.pennzoil.com**
Progressive Insurance, **www.progressive.com**
Quicken, **www.quicken.com**
State of Arkansas, **www.state.ar.us**
State of Connecticut, **www.state.ct.us**
State of Indiana, **www.state.in.us**
State of Pennsylvania, **www.state.pa.us**
State of Virginia, **www.state.va.us**
Surgeon General C. Everett Koop, **www.drkoop.com**
Useit.com, **www.useit.com**
Wal-Mart, **www.wal-mart.com**

Executive Presentations
by Jack Shaw

In order to share the concepts presented in this book, you may want to consider an executive briefing for your company or organization. A 60- to 90-minute briefing session will highlight most of the business management aspects of eBusiness and eCommerce covered in this book. Longer sessions are also available to cover these aspects in more detail.

Jack's most requested presentations:

Surviving the Digital Jungle

The Internet — The New Marketspace

Winning With eCommerce!

Short-term consulting is also available.

For more information please go to www.e-com.com or call 770.565.4010 and ask to receive a speaker kit with a preview video.

eCommerce Strategies, Inc.
2627 Sandy Plains Rd., Ste. 202
Marietta, GA 30066
770.565.4010
speaker@e-com.com

Ordering Information

You may order additional copies of **Surviving the Digital Jungle** by phone, fax, mail, or email. Single copies are $28 plus shipping and handling. Quantity discounts are available.

You will need to provide your name and shipping information, a credit card number with expiration date (or a check with mail orders), the title of the book, and the number of copies you wish to order.

Phone: 1.770.565.4010

Fax: 1.770.565.4062

Mail: 2627 Sandy Plains Rd., Ste. 202
Marietta, GA 30066

Email: digitaljungle@e-com.com